The Blues

Lucent Library of Black History

Other titles in this series:

The Blues

Lucent Library of Black History

Michael V. Uschan

LUCENT BOOKS

A part of Gale, Cengage Learning

Detroit • New York • San Francisco • New Haven, Conn • Waterville, Maine • London

LIBRARY OF CONGRESS CATALOGING-IN-PUBLICATION DATA

Uschan, Michael V., 1948-
  The blues / by Michael V. Uschan.
      p. cm. -- (Lucent library of Black history)
  Includes bibliographical references and index.
  ISBN 978-1-4205-0658-7 (hardcover)
  1. Blues (Music)--History and criticism--Juvenile literature. I. Title.
  ML3521.U83 2012
  781.64309--dc23
                                                              2011023800

Lucent Books
27500 Drake Rd.
Farmington Hills, MI 48331

ISBN-13: 978-1-4205-0658-7
ISBN-10: 1-4205-0658-7

Printed in the United States of America
1 2 3 4 5 6 7 15 14 13 12 11

Printed by Bang Printing, Brainerd, MN, 1st Ptg., 09/2011

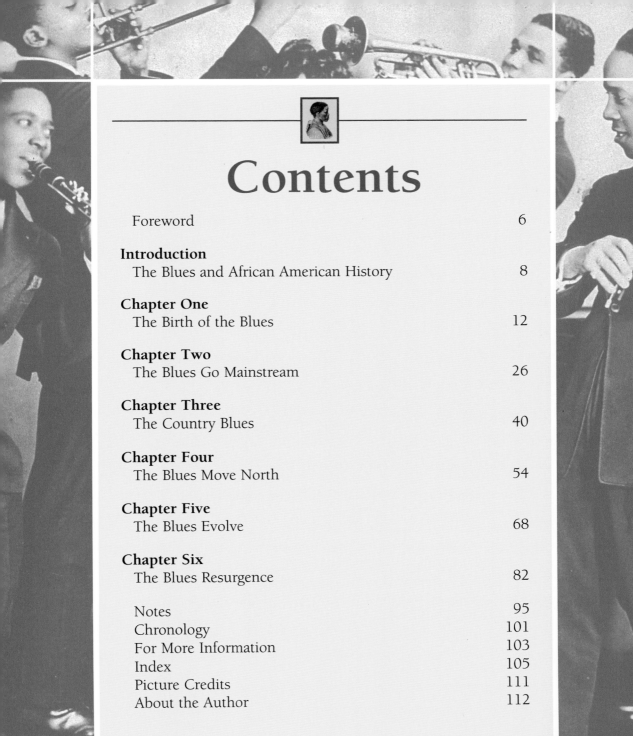

Contents

Foreword

It has been more than 500 years since Africans were first brought to the New World in shackles, and over 140 years since slavery was formally abolished in the United States. Over 50 years have passed since the fallacy of "separate but equal" was obliterated in the American courts, and some 40 years since the watershed Civil Rights Act of 1964 guaranteed the rights and liberties of all Americans, especially those of color. Over time, these changes have become celebrated landmarks in American history. In the twenty-first century, African American men and women are politicians, judges, diplomats, professors, deans, doctors, artists, athletes, business owners, and home owners. For many, the scars of the past have melted away in the opportunities that have been found in contemporary society. Observers such as Peter N. Kirsanow, who sits on the U.S. Commission of Civil Rights, point to these accomplishments and conclude, "The growing black middle class may be viewed as proof that most of the civil rights battles have been won."

In spite of these legal victories, however, prejudice and inequality have persisted in American society. In 2003, African Americans comprised just 12 percent of the nation's population, yet accounted for 44 percent of its prison inmates and 24 percent of its poor. Racially motivated hate crimes continue to appear on the pages of major newspapers in many American cities. Furthermore, many African Americans still experience either overt or muted racism in their daily lives. A 1996 study undertaken by Professor Nancy Krieger of the Harvard School of Public Health, for example, found that 80 percent of the African American participants reported having experienced racial discrimination in one or more settings, including at work or school, applying for housing and medical care, from the police or in the courts, and on the street or in a public setting.

It is for these reasons that many believe the struggle for racial equality and justice is far from over. These episodes of discrimination threaten to shatter the illusion that America has completely overcome its racist past, causing many black Americans to become increasingly frustrated and confused. Scholar and writer Ellis Cose has described this splintered state in the following way: "I have done everything I was supposed to do. I have stayed out of trouble with the law, gone to the right schools, and worked myself nearly to death. What more do they want? Why in God's name won't they accept me as a full human being?" For Cose and others, the struggle for equality and justice has yet to be fully achieved.

In many subtle yet important ways the traumatic experiences of slavery and segregation continue to inform the way race is discussed and experienced in the twenty-first century. Indeed, it is possible that America will always grapple with the fallout from its distressing past. Ulric Haynes, dean of the Hofstra University School of Business, has said, "Perhaps race will always matter, given the historical circumstances under which we came to this country." But studying this past and understanding how it contributes to present-day dialogues about race and history in America is a critical component of contemporary education. To this end, the Lucent Library of Black History offers a thorough look at the experiences that have shaped the black community and the American people as a whole. Annotated bibliographies provide readers with ideas for further research, while fully documented primary and secondary source quotations enhance the text. Each book in the series explores a different episode of black history; together they provide students with a wealth of information as well as launching points for further study and discussion.

The Blues and African American History

February 1, 2003, was a special date in the history of blues music. That day marked the beginning of the Year of the Blues, a celebration the U.S. Senate authorized to honor the popular genre of music. U.S. Senate Resolution 316 hailed the blues as "the most influential form of American roots music [and] a national historic treasure, which needs to be preserved, studied, and documented for future generations."[1] The Senate noted that throughout the preceding century, the blues had influenced many types of American music, including folk, country, jazz, and hip-hop. Rock and roll is considered a direct descendant of the blues.

No one knows when or where the blues originated, but among the earliest records of the music's existence is a recollection from African American composer W.C. Handy. In 1903 Handy was waiting for a train in Tutwiler, Mississippi, when a man began singing and playing what Handy termed "the weirdest music I'd ever heard."[2] Handy was a trained musician, but the song had a melody unlike anything he had ever heard. The song was a blues tune. Intrigued by the new music, Handy began composing and playing blues songs for the orchestra he led, and in 1912 his sheet music for "The Memphis Blues" was one of the first blues songs ever published.

Even though Handy did not invent the blues, he understood the inspiration for this unique style of music. In his 1941 autobiography, Handy wrote: "All of our [African American] music is derived from suffering. [During] slavery the suffering was a result of the lash and the cruel separation of families and loved ones. Today we suffer as a consequence of the past, through man's inhumanity to man [continuing racism against blacks]. Then as now our music was our consolation."[3]

African American Music

The blues that emerged in the late nineteenth century and became popular across the nation in the first few decades of the twentieth century were a culmination of two things: the musical traditions Africans brought with them when they were kidnapped from their homelands and sold into slavery in the New World, and the brutal treatment most African Americans received at the hands of whites for more than three centuries. Until the blues appeared in the late nineteenth century, American music generally mimicked traditional patterns of harmony and style created by European musicians, singers, and composers. But the blues and other types of music that blacks created was different. Blues historian Paul Oliver writes, "It is evident to the most casual listener that the blues [and] other forms of African American music have certain qualities that are [neither] familiar nor . . . as marked in the western traditions of either formal or folk music."[4]

The most notable way in which the blues differ from traditional European and early American music is its uneven, irregular rhythms and blue notes—notes that are sung or played at a slightly lower pitch than those of the typical European and American musical scale. Blues singers also departed from traditional European and American vocal styles by using vocal techniques common in Africa. The high-pitched wails, deep-throated moaning tones, and harsh grunts associated with African singing gave blues songs both emotional strength and a unique new artistic styling.

In an 1816 book Englishman George Pinckard wrote about the strange singing he overheard when blacks arrived in Savannah, Georgia, aboard a slave ship. He characterized their chanting songs as "a wild yell devoid of all softness and harmony, and loudly chant-

9

Although he did not invent the blues, W.C. Handy was the first to compose and play blues songs with his orchestra in 1912.

ed in harsh harmony."[5] In a series of newspaper articles in the late 1850s that helped turn many Northerners against slavery, journalist Frederick Law Olmsted described a song slaves sang as they worked: "Suddenly one [slave] raised such a sound as I had never heard before, a long, loud, musical shout rising and falling and breaking into falsetto, his voice ringing throughout the woods in the clear, frosty night air, like a bugle call. As he finished, the melody was caught up by another, and then another, and then by several in chorus."[6]

Another connection that the blues has to African traditions is that blues singers have been compared to griots, wandering musicians in Africa who even today compose songs and poems that comment on historical events and everyday life. Blues historian Francis Davis writes, "Now that Westerners know more about African culture, [blues] singers and guitarists are frequently likened to griots. Blues singers in the [Mississippi] Delta and elsewhere did serve as oral historians, conveyors of local myths."[7]

In addition to such African musical influences, however, there is another factor that makes the blues a distinctly African American music—its connection to the bitter treatment blacks have long endured in their new homeland.

Music Born of Misery

From the time the first African Americans arrived in 1619 in the English colony of Virginia until the Civil War ended in 1865, most blacks lived as slaves in the United States. The blues developed in southern states in the late nineteenth century. By this time slavery had ended, but whites still harshly oppressed blacks and denied them basic civil rights. Many early blues songs focused on the hardships of this racist treatment. In 1929 Bessie Tucker recorded "Mean Old Master," a song about an evil white man who bullied workers on his plantation. Tucker sang, "Our boss man may come here—we did not run; Oh master got a pistol, he have a great big gun."[8]

Another common blues theme is love. Some songs are filled with the joy of love and relationships, but even more express the pain of romantic betrayal, disappointment, or longing. The recurring theme of heartache makes some people think blues songs are always sad. In 1959, however, noted African American author Richard Wright explained that the blues is more than songs of despair. Wright wrote:

> The most astonishing aspect of blues is that, although replete with a sense of defeat and down-heartedness, they are not intrinsically pessimistic; their burden of woe and melancholy [also includes] an almost exultant affirmation of life, of love, [of] hope. No matter how repressive was the American environment, the Negro never lost faith in or doubted his deeply endemic capacity to live.[9]

Some blues songs celebrate life or poke fun at life's problems. In 1928 Robert "Barbecue Bob" Hicks sang proudly about his racial identity: "So glad I'm brown skin, So glad I'm brown skin, Chocolate to the bone."[10] During the Great Depression, Thomas A. "Georgia Tom" Dorsey joked that, like many other blacks, he had not lost much when the economy crashed and made many people poor for the first time: "I didn't feel so depressed, For I didn't have a thing to start with."[11]

The blues has changed greatly since Handy first heard it more than a century ago. Today musicians from many cultural backgrounds play and sing the blues, but the music is still intimately connected to the African American culture that inspired it.

Chapter One

The Birth of the Blues

The blues as it is known and loved today evolved from African American forms of music that were created over several hundred years. These musical ancestors of the blues included field hollers and work songs that slaves sang as they worked and the spirituals African Americans sang to praise God. *The Long Road to Freedom: An Anthology of Black Music* is a CD collection that traces how African American music evolved from the slave era to modern times. The collection includes African chants slaves brought with them to their new home, spirituals, and secular music like the blues. In an introduction to the set, African American entertainer Harry Belafonte explains how the various styles of music bear witness to the unique experience of blacks in America:

> Every song in this collection speaks to the experience of the journey that captives from Africa had to endure on the long road to freedom. In the beginning, our music was our source of hope, our well of truth. With the power and resources of white society directed at perpetuating the myth of our inferiority, we were in a constant struggle for truth about our heritage. Having no access to printing presses or centers of learning, we used music as a link to our history and as documents of our social and political experiences.[12]

As Belafonte notes, African American music as it is known today was shaped by the most brutal, dehumanizing aspect of U.S. history—slavery.

They Brought Their Music

African Americans are unlike most American ethnic groups in that, for most of them, their ancestors were forced to move to the United States instead of immigrating by choice. Abducted mainly from areas of western Africa, men, women, and children were placed in chains and marched onto slave ships against their will. They were transported across the Atlantic Ocean to be sold as slaves. Hundreds of thousands of blacks arrived with few possessions except memories of their homeland. However, they were sometimes allowed to take their musical instruments in hopes that this entertainment would help them survive the long, difficult journey from Africa. Some of the most important cultural traditions they retained were those relating to music, which played a central part in the lives of Africans.

After their arrival in America, slaves continued their musical traditions by playing for their fellow slaves and even whites.

One of the Africans forced into slavery was Olaudah Equiano, who was eleven when he was kidnapped from Guinea and taken to Virginia in 1756. Unlike most slaves, Equiano learned to read and write. Equiano was sold to a Quaker in Philadelphia and worked as a clerk in his master's shipping company. The Quaker paid him for his work and allowed him to purchase his freedom with the money he saved. Equiano moved to England in the late 1760s because he feared he might be enslaved again in the English colonies. His 1789 autobiography exposed the horrors of slavery and helped influence the English parliament in 1807 to abolish the slave trade, which continued in the United States for another half century. Equiano's autobiography explained the importance of music to Africans: "We might be called a people of dancers, musicians and poets, since important events such as a triumphant return from war or any other reason for popular rejoicing are celebrated by dancing accompanied by appropriate music and singing."[13]

On voyages from Africa, some ship captains allowed blacks to leave the dark, dirty holds in which they were confined to get sun and fresh air on the upper deck. When that happened, they often sang or used wooden tubs or other objects as makeshift instruments to create music. Some slaves continued to play music when they reached their new homes. They played music for their fellow slaves in their free time and were often ordered to play for whites. In his 1781 book *Notes on Virginia*, future president Thomas Jefferson suggested that African slaves were gifted musically, "with accurate ears for a tune and time and they have been found capable of imagining [composing] a small catch [song]."[14]

African Instruments

Jefferson described an African instrument slaves played called the "banjar"—it later became known as the banjo—which was made from hollowed-out gourds. Blacks also used another African instrument—dried animal bones that they clicked together to provide rhythm for their music. African Americans also knew how to play flutelike wind instruments, other stringed instruments similar to lutes, and drums, which were all common instruments in African culture. Slaves were originally allowed to play drums. But whites prohibited that practice when they discovered slaves had

A banjo from around 1800. Blacks brought to America an instrument called the banjar which would evolve into the American banjo.

developed complicated drumbeats to communicate with slaves at other plantations. Slave owners stopped them from using drums after they learned that slaves had been able to use drums to coordinate uprisings among slaves from different locations, something that happened many times before the owners realized what was happening.

Spirituals

———————————■———————————

Musical historian Burton W. Peretti explains how slaves used African musical traditions to create spirituals that were unlike any sacred music Americans had ever heard:

> Black spirituals were an identifiable genre of sacred music, indigenous to the slave South, which represented African Americans' emotional and sacred yearnings in an extraordinary manner. Spirituals originated when African American slaves borrowed from Baptist and Methodist [hymns]. They combined lines and memorable phrases from hymns with their own favorite Biblical parables and folk legends. Also, [black] preachers often broke into song during their sermons, repeating key phrases and lessons in a manner that evolved into makeshift call-and-response hymns. The creative reworking of standard hymns echoed the verbal skill of griots and other song specialists of West Africa. More than any other variety of slave music, the spirituals won the attention and admiration of white listeners. [Like] work songs, many of the spirituals were "sorrow songs," biblical expressions of grief, longing, and supplication that were all too applicable to the slave life. The famed titles of some of them convey these deep sentiments: "Sometimes I Feel Like a Motherless Child," "Trouble in Mind," "O Rock, Don't Fall on Me," "And the Moon Will Turn to Blood," "I've Been Rebuked and I've Been Scorned," and "Let My People Go."

Burton W. Peretti. *Lift Every* Voice: *The History of African American Music.* New York: Rowman and Littlefield, 2009, p. 28.

Although many slaves learned to play Western music, they also began creating new music and songs. Eileen Southern, the first African American female tenured full professor at Harvard University, extensively researched the history of black music. She wrote that slaves created music to deal with the horror of slavery: "The function of music as a communal activity [in Africa], for example, led to the development of slave-song repertoires that provided some measure of release from the physical and spiritual brutality of slavery."[15]

These new styles of music were hybrids of blacks' African heritage, their exposure to Western music, and the experiences they had endured as slaves.

Field Hollers and Sorrow Songs

Africans had traditionally sung communally while working in groups. Enslaved Africans continued the practice, inventing field hollers, or short chants they sang or shouted while laboring in fields in the American South. They also created more complicated work songs they sang while doing other types of labor. They perfected this singing in Southern plantations where large numbers of slaves cleared fields, dug canals, and harvested crops. Work songs used call-and-response, an African song style evident in many types of black music, including the blues. Call-and-response helped the leader of a group of slaves keep everyone working at the same pace. The songs began with a statement sung or shouted by a lead vocalist followed by a response from other workers. This style can be seen in the work song "Go Down Old Hannah," which goes in part: "Leader: Go down Old Hannah. Group: Go down Old Hannah! Leader: And don't you rise no more: Group: And don't you rise no more."[16] This is an example of a work song that had a special meaning for slaves. "Old Hannah" was a nickname for the sun. The slaves were expressing their discontent about working from sunrise to sunset in a sort of code, so they would not be punished for complaining.

Some work songs had rhythms that helped blacks keep a steady pace at various tasks like cutting sugarcane. But David "Honeyboy" Edwards, a famed blues musician and singer, explains that such songs also made the labor more enjoyable: "In slave times, working all day, they had to sing songs [to make] the day pass by easier."[17]

Spirituals were another early form of black music. Spirituals were similar to traditional hymns whites sang but had elements of African music such as call-and-response. This new type of church music developed because slaves began changing words and melodies of white worship songs to suit their musical tastes. Blues historian Amiri Baraka stresses, "The lyrics, rhythms, and even the harmonies were essentially of African derivation [and] the spirituals themselves were probably the first completely native American music the slaves made."[18] Spirituals were also called "sorrow songs" because they expressed the pain blacks felt at being slaves.

Spirituals and other songs blacks composed sometimes contained secret messages about escaping slavery. The foremost example of what are called coded songs is the spiritual "Wade in the Water." The title itself is a tip to slaves that walking through a river or stream will help escaping slaves hide their scent from whites tracking them with dogs. Southern wrote that blacks sometimes changed song lyrics to inform fellow slaves about escape attempts: "It is possible that when an escape plot was in the air, traditional songs were provided with parody verses specifically stating meeting places and departure times."[19] Coded songs were also used by the Underground Railroad, the group of antislavery whites and blacks who helped slaves escape to Northern states, where slavery had been outlawed.

Whites who overheard blacks singing, even slaves toiling at arduous labor, often believed the songs meant the slaves were happy. But Frederick Douglass, a Maryland slave who escaped to freedom in 1838 at the age of twenty and became a leader of the movement to abolish slavery, said that was false. He wrote: "It is a great mistake to suppose them happy because they sing the songs for the slave [songs] represent the sorrow, rather than the joys, of his heart; and he is relieved by them, only as an aching heart is relieved by tears."[20]

The music slaves made to ease their existence took many forms.

Other Black Music

Almost every plantation had musically talented slaves who could perform either African American or European American music, and their masters often forced them to perform for white guests at parties or dances. However, slave owners had to make sure they knew what songs black musicians would perform for white audiences. That was because slaves often made up songs that poked fun at whites. In 1774 Nicholas Cresswell, a visitor from England, wrote, "[In] their songs they generally relate the usage they have received from their Masters or Mistresses in a very satirical manner." Although Cresswell characterized the songs as "rude and uncultivated,"[21] so many whites enjoyed various forms of black music that a new form of entertainment was created—minstrel shows.

Minstrel Shows

In the first half of the nineteenth century, minstrel shows, also called minstrelsy, became the most widespread, popular form of mass entertainment in the United States. Minstrel shows exploited the popularity of black music and entertainment to create racist caricatures of African Americans. Music historian Eileen Southern explained that there were two main ways white minstrels parodied black life:

> Blackface minstrelsy was a form of theatrical performance that emerged during the 1820s and reached its zenith during the years 1850–70. Essentially it consisted of an exploitation of the slave's style of music and dancing by white men, who blackened their faces with burnt cork and went on the stage to sing "Negro songs" (also called "Ethiopian songs"), to perform dances derived from those of the slaves, and to tell jokes based on slave life. Two basic types of slave impersonations were developed: one in caricature of the plantation slave with his ragged clothes and thick dialect; the other portraying the city slave, the dandy dressed in the latest fashion, who boasted of his exploits among the ladies. The former was referred to as Jim Crow and the latter as Zip Coon.

Eileen Southern. *The Music of Black Americans: A History.* New York: Norton, 1997, p. 89.

Starting in the 1820s white entertainers began wearing blackface in minstrel shows. Enormously popular, the shows reinforced black stereotypes with racist jokes and skits to make blacks look lazy, ignorant, and immoral.

In the 1820s white entertainers began performing black songs, jokes, and dances in traveling revues called minstrel shows; they were also called minstrelsy. Although the shows started because many whites enjoyed black entertainment, the whites' versions of the songs and dances were racist in tone and mocked slaves. Performers were whites who smeared their faces with burned cork to make themselves look black, and their songs and skits portrayed blacks as ignorant, lazy, and immoral. One of the minstrel originators was Thomas Dartmouth "Daddy" Rice, a white actor from New York who in 1828 developed a song-and-dance routine that mocked the antics of a crippled slave. By the late 1840s such shows had become the nation's most popular form of entertainment.

Many historians and commentators agree that the racist portrayal of blacks helped whites justify slavery as well as their right to continue to dominate blacks after slavery was completely abolished in 1865. Says Belafonte: "The image of the lazy, shiftless [black] buffoon would be our burden for almost a century."[22] Nonetheless, African Americans started to portray themselves in minstrel shows. In the 1840s William Henry Lane and Thomas Dilward became the first African Americans to perform in minstrel shows—and by 1855 there were many touring African American minstrel groups.

The popularity of minstrel shows waned during the Civil War. When the North defeated the South, African Americans were not only freed from slavery but freed to create new forms of music. One of them was the blues.

The Mysterious Origin of the Blues

There is no historical evidence to pinpoint when and where African Americans first began singing and playing songs that eventually became known as the blues. But the style began to emerge in the Mississippi Delta region and other southern states in the last few decades of the nineteenth century. Sadness, even despair, was an element of many of those early songs. Since one meaning of the word *blue* is that a person is melancholy or depressed, that is the most likely explanation for why the music was named "the blues." African American poet, playwright, and blues historian Baraka writes that during this period, African Americans were often justified in feeling sad: "The blues was conceived by freedmen and ex-slaves—if not as the result of a personal or intellectual experience, at least as an emotional confirmation of, and reaction to, the way in which most Negroes were still forced to exist in the United States."[23]

Although blacks rejoiced in their new freedom when the Civil War ended, that happiness was crushed in the next few decades as they realized that the end of slavery had not given them equality. Whites continued to deny blacks basic rights like being able to vote and restricted their access to jobs and resources. Whites used

The Delta Blues Museum in Clarksdale, Mississippi, chronicles the beginning of the blues in the Mississippi Delta region.

W.C. Handy

William Christopher Handy was born November 16, 1873, in Florence, Alabama. Handy was a trained musician, and the bands he led played conventional music. When Handy first heard a blues song in 1903, he dismissed the music as primitive. But two years later in Cleveland, Mississippi, a ragged group of blues musicians asked to play some songs so members of his band could take a break. The crowd liked the music so much that they threw lots of money at the raggedly dressed musicians, so Handy decided to start writing and playing blues tunes. In his 1941 autobiography *Father of the Blues*, the nickname he earned by helping to popularize the blues, Handy explains this turning point in his life:

> A rain of silver dollars began to fall around the outlandish, stomping feet. The dancers went wild. Dollars, quarters, halves—the shower grew heavier and continued so long I strained my neck to get a better look. There before the boys lay more money than my nine musicians were being paid for the entire engagement. Then I saw the beauty of primitive music. They had the stuff the people wanted. Their music wanted polishing [but] folks would pay for it. The old conventional music was well and good and had its place, no denying that, but there was no virtue in being blind when you had good eyes.

> W.C. Handy. *Father of the Blues: An Autobiography of W.C. Handy*. New York: Macmillan, 1941, p. 77.

W.C. Handy was a young musician when he heard his first blues song, played by a black guitarist at a railroad station in Tutwiller, Mississippi.

violence and political and economic power to dominate blacks. This was especially true in the South, where 90 percent of blacks lived.

Southern states created laws that segregated the races and made it very difficult for African Americans to get an education. White control of the economy limited the type of jobs blacks could hold, which kept most blacks poor, and white-run justice systems unfairly punished blacks for minor offenses. In what amounted to a new form of slavery, southern prisons allowed whites to hire black inmates as laborers. To ensure a supply of cheap labor, white justice officials often sentenced blacks to prison for minor or nonexistent crimes. A blues tune in the early twentieth century, when white courts were still discriminating against blacks, summed up the misery of people who were unfairly imprisoned: "They got me accused of murder and I haven't harmed a man, They got me accused of forgery and I can't write my name."[24]

Injustice was a common theme of many blues songs. But W.C. Handy, known as the "Father of the Blues," claims, "Southern Negroes sang about everything. Trains, steam whistles, sledge hammers, fast women, mean bosses, stubborn mules—all became subjects for their songs."[25] Befitting their new station as free people, these songs included ballads that had black heroes. The most famous was John Henry, a black worker who defeated a machine in a contest to dig a tunnel, only to die from his heroic exertions.

Blues music was carried throughout the South by black musicians who, once freed from slavery, began traveling to see as many new places as they could. Southern wrote, "The early anonymous singers of the blues often were wanderers [who] carried their plaintive songs from one black community to another."[26] These first bluesmen traveled on horses and mules, by foot, and often by railroad, either as passengers or by stealing rides in freight cars. It was therefore no surprise that Handy first encountered the blues in a railroad station.

Handy Hears the Blues

Handy was an African American musician and bandleader trained in conventional European American music. In 1903 while he was waiting for a train in Tutwiler, Mississippi, Handy heard a black man playing the guitar and singing a song—it was the first blues tune Handy ever heard. Handy described the historic encounter in his 1941 autobiography:

> A lean, loose-jointed Negro had commenced plunking a guitar beside me while I slept. His clothes were rags; his feet peeped out of his shoes. His face had on it some of the sadness of the ages. As he played, he pressed a knife on the strings of the guitar in a manner popularized by Hawaiian guitarists who used steel bars. The effect was unforgettable. His song, too, struck me instantly. "Goin' where the Southern cross' the Dog." The singer repeated the line three times, accompanying himself on the guitar [and] the tune stayed on my mind.[27]

Railroads were a popular subject for early blues tunes because of the novelty of travel for blacks—"Southern" and "Dog" were nicknames for train lines whose tracks crossed. Handy admitted that at first the music seemed simplistic to him: "As a director of many respectable, conventional bands [I] was not ready to believe that this was just what the public wanted."[28] But two years later in Cleveland, Mississippi, Handy realized the music's popularity when he saw how much money a group of blacks made by playing the blues. The incident led Handy to incorporate blues music into the repertoire of bands he led.

The early blues had a standardized format in which the song opened with one line repeated twice, followed by a third line that finished the theme of the first two. An example is "Boll Weevil, where you been so Long!; Boll Weevil, where you been so Long!; You stole my cotton, now you want my corn."[29] Many blues songs were written about boll weevils because the devastation the bugs caused to crops could ruin the lives of farmers in the South. The lyric structure known as AAB was found in most early blues songs. The early blues became known as twelve-bar blues because the melodies were uniformly standardized. The term *twelve-bar* refers to the number of measures, or musical bars, in the melody of a song. Nearly all blues music is also played to a four-four time signature, which means there are four beats in every measure or bar, and each quarter note is equal to one beat.

Handy borrowed that musical structure and began writing his own blues songs, which became so popular that they helped to establish the blues as an important new music style. In a 1923 interview, Handy noted that the blues owed its development to black music of the past: "They are essentially racial [and each] of my blues is based on some old Negro song of the South, some folk-song that I heard from my mammy when I was a child. Something that sticks in my mind, that I hum to myself when I'm not thinking about it. Some old song that is a part of the memories of my childhood and of my race."[30]

Chapter Two

The Blues Go Mainstream

Until the early twentieth century, blues songs were sung in anonymity by poor blacks living in southern states. It was not until black musicians began formally publishing their songs and putting them on records and their songs began to be played on the radio that people throughout the nation had a chance to appreciate the new style of music.

One of the first musicians to bring blues music to mainstream audiences was W.C. Handy. In 1909 Handy wrote a campaign song with a blues melody for E.H. Crump, a mayoral candidate in Memphis, Tennessee. African Americans throughout their musical history have often created songs that mocked whites. In that tradition Handy wrote a set of lyrics for the song that ridiculed Crump's promise to reform saloon entertainment. The lyrics, which were only sung in black establishments, included the line "We don't care what Mr. Crump don' low [allow]; We gon' to bar'l-house [barrelhouse was a spirited piano style of blues] anyhow."[31]

Handy later wrote new lyrics for the tune and retitled it "The Memphis Blues." Published in 1912, it was one of the first blues songs set down on paper so people living outside the South could learn about, hear, and play the blues. In 1914

Handy's "The Saint Louis Blues" became a huge hit. Written about a woman mourning a boyfriend who left her, the song included the lyrics "I got them St. Louis blues, just as blue as I can be; He got a heart like a rock cast in the sea; Or else he would not go so far from me."[32]

In 1914 W.C. Handy's "The Saint Louis Blues" became the first blues song to be a big hit.

Publication of blues songs was the first step in helping to spread their popularity across the nation. But interest in the new style of music exploded in the 1920s with the release of the first blues records.

A New Record Market

Record companies in the early twentieth century shunned the blues. When Handy first suggested to companies that they record black female singers, white executives turned him down by claiming that either "their diction was different from white girls" or "they couldn't possibly fill the bill."[33] The executives did not understand the music's growing popularity and were afraid they would lose money on records aimed at a black audience.

American blues singer Mamie Smith poses with her band in New York City in 1920. She was the first African American woman to record a blues song.

That reluctance to deal with black singers ended after Okeh Records in New York City recorded an African American woman, Mamie Smith, on February 14, 1920, singing two romantic songs—"That Thing Called Love" and "You Can't Keep a Good Man Down." When the record sold ten thousand copies, the company brought Smith back on August 10, 1920, to record "Crazy Blues." In the tune about an unhappy love relationship, Smith crooned, "I can't sleep at night, I can't eat a bite; 'Cause the man I love, he don't treat me right; Now I got the crazy blues since my baby went away."[34] The first recorded blues song sold an astonishing seventy-five thousand copies in one month even though it cost one dollar, a lot of money at the time. The record's success made other companies recognize the popularity of the blues, and they began recording other female blues singers.

Blues and other African American music recordings became known as "race records." Okeh even established a separate label for black music called Original Race Records. The company's advertisements proudly proclaimed: "Who first thought of getting out Race records for the Race? Okeh, that's right. Genuine Race artists making Genuine Blues for Okeh."[35] In 1921 Black Swan, the first black-owned record company, countered by stating that it was "the Only Genuine Colored Record Company. Others Are Only Passing for Colored."[36]

In the next decade more than two hundred women recorded songs. Alberta Hunter, one of the biggest stars, once said, "[Smith] made it possible for all of us."[37] The success of Smith's recording of "Crazy Blues" proved there was a huge market for black music. And that new market, composed mainly of blacks living in northern cities, had been created by one of the nation's most historic population shifts—the Great Migration.

The Great Migration

In 1900 the nation's African American population numbered just under 10.5 million, with nearly 9 million blacks living in southern states. But from 1910 to 1930, 2 million blacks migrated to other states, mostly in the Midwest and Northeast. Most blacks wound up living in large cities like Chicago, New York, and Detroit, whose African American population swelled from 6,000 in 1910 to 120,000 in two decades.

Jazz and the Blues

Jazz originated in the early twentieth century—the term *jazz* itself was not used to refer to the music until about 1915 in Chicago. Because the blues began earlier, in the late nineteenth century, and because both originated in the South, the blues is believed to have been one of the major influences in the development of jazz. Jazz and the blues share several African musical traditions such as the use of blue notes, polyrhythms, and syncopation. The two musical styles share another important trait—the willingness of singers to invent new lyrics and the way they deliver them and the creativity of musicians in improvising new musical flourishes within the song's melody. Jazz and the blues have had a close relationship for more than a century, but music historian Earl L. Stewart claims it was never closer than when classic blues singers allowed jazz influences to shape some of their songs:

> The jazz styles and blues styles have traversed collateral developments marked by independent co-existence [and] symbiosis. The earliest intercourse between the two fused the style of jazz with the form and structure of the blues, and introduced to American vernacular music the most technically sophisticated of all blues styles—that is, the jazz blues [classic blues]. The jazz blues exemplifies a much greater stylistic and harmonic flexibility than what is typically found in other blues genres.

Earl L. Stewart. *Black Music: An Introduction.* New York: Schirmer, 1998, p. 5.

The Great Migration, which created the first significant black presence in cities outside the South, was triggered by the start of World War I in Europe in 1914. The United States did not enter the war until April 6, 1917, but the conflict's start created millions of jobs as U.S. companies began manufacturing guns, tanks, and other war materiel for England and France. For more than a century, European immigrants had provided a steady flow of new U.S. workers, but the war drastically reduced immigration, with the number of European immigrants falling from 1.3 million in 1914 to just over 100,000 one year later. That downturn created a labor shortage, one that was magnified when millions of men enlisted in the U.S. Army and Navy to fight in the war.

The dire demand for workers gave African Americans a chance to leave the South, because they were now assured of finding work. Most were happy to go, because southern racism made their lives miserable. Blues piano player Charles "Cow Cow" Davenport, who left Alabama in the 1920s, wrote a blues song that explained why blacks fled the South: "I'm tired of being Jim Crowed, gonna leave this Jim Crow town; Doggone my black soul, I'm sweet Chicago bound; Yes, sir, I'm leavin' here, from this ole Jim Crow town."[38]

The term *Jim Crow* came from "Jump Jim Crow," a minstrel song made popular by blackface performer Thomas Dartmouth "Daddy" Rice. The phrase became synonymous with the segregated

The term *Jim Crow* derives from the minstrel song "Jump Jim Crow" by Thomas Dartmouth Rice. For blacks it became synonymous with the segregated lifestyle and racist treatment blacks endured in the South for a century after slavery ended.

lifestyle and racist treatment southern blacks endured for a century after slavery ended. Jim Crow laws segregated blacks, barring them from entering businesses like restaurants and movie theaters reserved for whites. Under Jim Crow, white government officials established black schools that were inferior to white schools and denied blacks basic civil rights. White economic and political power combined with white violence by groups like the Ku Klux Klan to control blacks and keep them from fighting back to better their lives. In 1916 the *Chicago Defender* newspaper ran advertisements urging blacks to move north: "Every black man for the sake of his wife and daughter should leave, even at a financial sacrifice, every spot in the South where his worth is not appreciated enough to give him the standing of a man and a citizen in the community."[39]

There was less racial discrimination outside the South, which meant African Americans enjoyed greater personal freedom and could get better jobs to improve their economic standing. The greater spending power of blacks outside the South was a major reason record companies started making blues records, and the result was that the music spread to the entire nation.

Classic Blues

Most blues records in the 1920s featured female singers in what today is called classic blues. In their 1926 book on black music, Howard W. Odum and Guy B. Johnson admitted, "The majority of these formal blues are sung from the point of view of women [and] among the blues singers who have gained a more or less national recognition there is scarcely a man's name to be found."[40] The authors labeled the songs "formal blues" because they deviated in style significantly from earlier blues songs.

The blues that emerged in the rural South was usually performed by blacks with untrained voices and cheap musical accompaniment. The most popular instrument was the guitar, which was inexpensive, easy to play, and allowed solo performances. Although most blues singers were male, ragtime pianist Ferdinand Joseph "Jelly Roll Morton" LaMothe remembered watching Mamie Desdoumes play in New Orleans in 1902 despite a disfigured hand: "Two middle fingers of her right hand had been cut off, so she played the blues with only three fingers on her right hand."[41]

Bessie Smith was one of the first singers to take blues to the next level. She had a more sophisticated singing style than earlier blues singers and was backed by big bands that included piano, trumpet, clarinet, trombone, saxophone, and drums.

Most blues singers played the guitar, banjo, piano, or harmonica, and some singers were backed by musicians playing homemade instruments like stone jugs and washboards.

Female blues singers like Bessie Smith had more sophisticated singing styles and musical accompaniment than those first blues singers. Like most classic blues singers, Smith had performed professionally for years in touring tent shows, theaters, and cabarets before she started singing the blues. Historian Eileen Southern wrote, "The blueswomen were consummate entertainers who knew how to put over a song, the anguish of love, jealousy, revenge, bad luck, and the other things that were important in the lives of city women."[42] Some women sang accompanied by a piano, but most were backed by small bands that included instruments like a clarinet, trumpet, trombone, saxophone, and drums.

It was not just the number of instruments but the style in which the accompanying musicians played that made the songs different from earlier blues. Instead of a simple beat and melody provided by one instrument, groups backing singers like Smith used a variety of instruments and played more complex music. The musical style of the blues records was no secret—copies of "Crazy Blues" state that the record featured "Mamie Smith and Her Jazz Hounds." Her backup musicians played jazz, a black music style derived from the blues.

African American poet, playwright, and blues historian Amiri Baraka states emphatically, "Blues is the parent of all legitimate jazz."[43] Jazz is a combination of American and African musical traditions that surfaced in the early twentieth century after the blues had already been established. Although early blues songs had simple melodies usually played by one instrument, jazz was a more complex musical style that featured several instruments playing at the same time. One of the African musical traits that set jazz apart from European-influenced American music is polyrhythm, an overall sound created by multiple beats musicians play on various instruments. Classic blues was sung with jazz musical overtones because its singers were familiar with jazz from their previous musical careers in which they had sung many types of songs. Bessie Smith commented once on how jazz had influenced her: "I sang everything from blues to popular songs in a jazz style."[44]

Smith's elegant delivery was even more jazz oriented than other classic blues singers. Yet her songs still followed the blues format, and she instilled in them all the emotional power that made the blues so popular. And despite their refined accompaniment, most classic blues singers were close to the original spirit of the blues in their delivery. One of them was Gertrude "Ma" Rainey, who became known as the "Mother of the Blues" for her many hit songs.

Classic Blues Stars

Rainey—she hated her nickname and preferred being called "Madame" instead of "Ma"—was born Gertrude Pridgett on April 26, 1886, in Columbus, Georgia. She began performing as a teenager and became Ma Rainey in 1904 after marrying entertainer "Pa" Will Rainey. The couple toured with black revues like F.S. Wolcott's Rabbit Foot Minstrels and later had their own group— Rainey and Rainey, Assassinators of the Blues. Rainey told music historian John Work she first heard the blues in 1902 in a small Missouri town while traveling with a tent show. In his 1940 book, *American Negro Songs*, Work wrote, "[Rainey] tells of a girl from

Whites Listen to the Blues

The blues began attracting white fans in the 1920s. However, the divide between the two races was still a big one because many whites from northern areas had never mixed socially with blacks. One attraction of the blues for many whites was that the singers, their songs, and even the way they moved onstage seemed exotic and thrilling. Carl Van Vechten wrote several articles about Bessie Smith for *Vanity Fair* magazine. His account of a 1926 performance by Smith in Newark, New Jersey, is a disturbing mix of adoration and astonishment, as if the entertainer he is describing is from another planet:

> The hangings parted and a great brown woman emerged. [She was] very large and she wore a rose satin robe, spangled with sequins, which swept away from her trim ankles. Her face was beautiful with the rich ripe beauty of southern darkness, a deep brazen brown, matching the bronze of her bare arms. She walked slowly to the footlights. Then she began her strange rites in a voice full of shoutin' and moanin' and prayin' and sufferin', a wild, rough, Ethiopian voice, harsh and volcanic, but seductive and sensuous, too, released between rouged lips and the whitest of teeth, the singer swaying lightly to the rhythm as is the Negro custom.

Angela Y. Davis. *Blues Legacies and Black Feminism: Gertrude "Ma" Rainey, Bessie Smith, and Billie Holiday*. New York: Pantheon, 1998, p. 142.

the town who came to the tent one morning and began to sing about the 'man who left her.'" Rainey liked the music and began singing similar songs, which became popular with her fans. Work wrote that after people asked Rainey repeatedly what the new style of music was called, "one day she replied, in a moment of inspiration, 'It's the blues.'"[45]

Historian Angela Y. Davis claims Rainey became the first black woman "superstar" because her songs expressed the feelings of average blacks. In "Poor Man Blues" the lyrics "Mister rich man, rich man, open up your heart and mind; Give the poor man a chance, help stop these hard, hard times" struck a chord with African American suffering from widespread poverty. Rainey was also able to appeal directly to women with songs advising them to be independent in love relationships: "Trust no man, no further than your eyes can see; I said, trust no man, no further than your

Ma Rainey with her band in the early 1920s. Rainey may have been the first black "superstar" because her songs related to the feelings of average blacks.

eyes can see; He'll tell you that he loves you and swear it is true; The very next minute he'll turn his back on you."[46]

Rainey's style was simpler than that of Bessie Smith, but her rich voice and the emotional pull she created for listeners made her popular despite the fact that she was short, fat, and considered homely if not ugly. Baraka claims Rainey was "one of the most imitated and influential classic blues singers, and perhaps the one who can be called the link between the earlier, less polished blues styles and the smoother theatrical style of most of the later [blues] singer."[47] Her biggest challenger was Smith, whom the older Rainey had tutored in singing in 1912 when they toured together.

Smith was born in 1894 in Chattanooga, Tennessee. Tall and beautiful, Smith was dubbed the "Empress of the Blues," and she dressed like it. For shows, Smith donned expensive jewelry, gaudy costumes, and headdresses with as many as one thousand feathers. Her first record in 1923, "Down Hearted Blues," sold 1 million copies. Music historian Eileen Southern wrote that the secret of Smith's success was that "her blues had the earthiness and raw intensity of [older] blues despite her sophistication."[48] Like other female singers, her songs often mocked black males: "I've had a man for fifteen years, give him his room and board; Once he was like a Cadillac, now he's like an old, worn-out Ford."[49] The fearless way Smith attacked men in her songs mirrored her own personality—she had a reputation for challenging men, even racist whites. Smith biographer Chris Albertson describes an encounter Smith had in 1927 with white-robed Ku Klux Klan members who began pulling up wooden stakes to collapse the tent in which she was performing:

> [Smith] ran toward the intruders, stopped within ten feet of them, placed one hand on her hip and shook a clenched fist at the Klansmen. "What [do] you think you're doin'," she shouted above the sound of the band. "I'll get the whole damn tent out here if I have to. You just pick up them sheets and run!" The Klansmen, apparently too surprised to move, just stood there and gawked. Bessie hurled obscenities at them until they finally turned and disappeared quietly into the darkness.[50]

Ma Rainey

In 1984 the play *Ma Rainey's Black Bottom* (the title is one of Rainey's most famous songs) opened on Broadway. In an article about the play, author Sandra G. Shannon discussed Rainey's importance to blacks during the classic blues period:

> The play's namesake, Gertrude Pridgett "Ma" Rainey, provides a powerful symbol of the tensions felt by thousands of African Americans who became part of the massive post–World War I exodus north known as the Great Migration. Her popularity in Northern cities during the mid- to late 1920s was supported largely by Southern blacks, who found in her blues songs solace from the alienation and disillusionment of city life. Her down-home, earthy style, her naughty lyrics, and her rugged looks were welcomed by weary Southern blacks, no longer impressed by the deceptive glamour of the North. Her blues, therefore, was a gift to her people, for she intimately understood their miseries.

Sandra G. Shannon. "The Long Wait: August Wilson's 'Ma Rainey's Black Bottom.'" *Black American Literature Forum*, Spring 1991, p. 135

The play *Ma Rainey's Black Bottom* on Broadway with Charles Dutton and Whoopi Goldberg as Ma Rainey.

Other classic blues stars included Victoria Spivey, Sippie Wallace, Clara Smith, and Ethel Waters. Their records sound dated and antiquated compared to blues songs people hear today. But women who sang those songs nearly a century ago exerted a powerful influence on the development of the blues, one that is still being felt. Blues artist Koko Taylor's illustrious career began with the 1965 hit "Wang Dang Doodle." Taylor has said her own musical career was inspired by records of those singers she listened to while growing up in Shelby County, Tennessee: "I always said I would like to be like these people I'm hearing on these records. What these women did—like Ma Rainey—they was the foundation of the blues. They brought the blues up from slavery up to today."[51]

Chapter Three

The Country Blues

The blues were made popular in the 1920s not only by records but by an exciting new technology that was revolutionizing mass communication—radio. The first radio shows for entertainment purposes began airing in 1920, the same year Mamie Smith recorded the first blues song. The growth of radio was so phenomenal that by 1923, classic blues star Ida Cox was singing a song that showed how powerful people believed the new medium had become: "Mr. Radio Announcer, please listen to my plea; Turn on your radio and find my man for me."[52]

By creating more blues fans, radio shows forced record companies to find new stars. With a limited number of female singers available, companies began looking for singers in the South, where the blues originated. They discovered male singers, many of whom had been performing in obscurity and near poverty before being chosen to make records.

One of the first male stars was Lemon Jefferson, who, before he began recording, had earned his living on the streets of Dallas, Texas, by playing and singing for tips. Sightless since birth, he was known as "Blind" Lemon Jefferson. Other male recording stars in the 1920s and early 1930s included "Papa" Charlie Jackson, Lonnie Johnson, Charley Patton, Eddie "Son" House, and Robert Johnson.

By 1923 classic blues star Ida Cox was singing the blues on the new medium of radio to a nationwide audience.

A New-Old Blues

Blind Lemon and other male blues singers were the first to record country blues, a style that had been played in the South for decades but was rarely heard outside that region until the 1920s. Music historian David Evans claims Jefferson did more than any

Blind Blues Singers

From "Blind" Lemon Jefferson in the 1920s to Ray Charles and Stevie Wonder decades later, there have been many great blind singers of the blues. Music historian Christopher John Farley explains why so many sightless singers have had success in this musical genre:

> Blind Lemon Jefferson was one of history's most important blues figures—but he was far from the only significant sightless blues performer. [Others include] Blind Willie Johnson, Blind Willie McTell, Reverend Blind Gary Davis, Blind Blake, Blind Boy Fullers [and at least one woman] blues gospel singer Arizona Dranes. Over the years there has been a lot of speculation in blues circles about exactly why there seem to be so many blind blues performers. One answer [is] that when one was blind, black, and living in the rural South [in the early twentieth century] there are few options, professionally speaking, besides going into music. Another argument, perhaps the most persuasive, is that blind performers, whose focus by nature is on the senses they have remaining, are more suited to master an aural and oral discipline such as the blues.

Peter Guralnick, Robert Santelli, Holly George-Warren, and Christopher John Farley, eds. *Martin Scorsese Presents the Blues: A Musical Journey.* New York: Amistad, 2003, p. 164.

"Blind" Willie McTell was a consummate Georgia bluesman who used the twelve-string guitar to play the blues. He wrote and recorded many great blues songs, among them "Statesboro Blues," in the 1920s and 30s.

early male star to popularize the traditional style that predated classic blues. Evans writes:

> Although a few other guitar-playing bluesmen had made records before Blind Lemon Jefferson, it is he who wears the crown for being the first popular star of [country] blues [because of his] spectacular reception by African-American record buyers. His commercial success opened the door to recording opportunities for hundreds of other guitar-playing blues singers.[53]

Jefferson recorded his first two songs—"Booster Blues" and "Dry Southern Blues"—in March 1926 for Paramount Records. Blues historian Tom Piazza explains that Jefferson's rough vocals and virtuoso guitar playing were a sharp contrast to the refined singing and jazz-influenced accompaniment of classic blues: "They were much rawer and closer to the rural sound of the field holler than anything that had ever been put on record. Jefferson was a great singer, and the wailing melodic line of his high, piercing voice was supported by a constant and extraordinarily inventive commentary from his guitar."[54]

Jefferson typified country blues singers in the second half of the 1920s. Like Jefferson, most accompanied themselves musically—usually on acoustic guitar, although a few played banjo or harmonica. Blues historian Eileen Southern wrote that the way the men sang also set them apart from the women: "The voice quality was strained, raspy, abrasive, nasal, fierce; there was a great deal of falsetto, humming, growling—whatever it took to sing the lament or tell the story." Southern also said their accompaniment had a primitive, visceral power that was like nothing many people had ever heard:

> [They] slapped their instruments, stomped their feet, and beat the strings of the guitar, producing a percussive effect. And they worked out special devices—drawing the blade of a broken bottle-neck or a brass ring or a piece of polished bone slipped over the finger—to produce whining tones reminiscent of the human voice, so that their instrument could "talk" to them.[55]

Another hallmark of country blues was that the African musical element of syncopation was more pronounced than in the smoother classic blues. African American music historian Earl L. Stewart explains syncopation: "The essential rhythmic characteristic of virtually all African American [music] styles is syncopation; the accenting (emphasizing) of rhythmic patterns on weak rather than strong pulses. In other words, syncopated rhythms give a feeling of temporality contradicting the strong beats of the prevailing measure."[56]

The uneven stressing of words produces ragged beats that are a key element of the blues as well as modern music that stemmed from it such as rock and roll. Thus, when Jefferson sang, "If I don't find my baby now, they're gonna hafta' bury me,"[57] he stressed "bury" instead of "me," which would be typical in European American music.

Blind Lemon

Although Jefferson was the first country blues singer to achieve stardom, his road to fame was unusual. Lemon Henry Jefferson was born on September 24, 1893, in Coutchman, Texas. Jefferson claimed he was blind from birth, but some biographers claim he might have been able to see well enough to make out large shapes and objects. Unable to perform manual labor, one of the few jobs open to blacks in that era, Jefferson and many other blind African Americans turned to music as a way to earn a living. In one of his songs, "Blind" Willie McTell once ironically sang, "I got the blues so bad, I can feel them in the dark."[58]

By the time Jefferson was in his teens, he was making money playing at picnics and parties and working as a street musician in various cities. Samuel Price was a black pianist who worked in a Dallas music store in the 1920s. He once recalled, "In Dallas, [Jefferson] used to spend every day walking from one end of town to the other, playing and singing in the street and in various taverns for tips."[59] When Price heard that Paramount was seeking blues singers, he recommended Jefferson, and the company brought Jefferson to Chicago.

The first recording date Paramount set up was on a Sunday in either December 1925 or January 1926, but to the surprise of company executives, Jefferson refused to sing any blues. Offered ten dollars a song, Jefferson stated: "I couldn't play it if you give me $200. I need the money, but I couldn't play it. My mother

Blind from birth "Blind" Lemon Jefferson was among the first bluesmen to record country blues and take it out of the south to where it could be heard nationwide.

always told me not to play on Sunday for nobody. Today is Sunday."[60] Jefferson did sing two religious songs, which were issued under the name Deacon L.J. Bates. In March 1926, presumably on a day other than a Sunday, Jefferson recorded some blues songs, and in May his "Got the Blues" became his first big hit.

Jefferson composed most of his songs. Blues historian Giles Oakley writes that Jefferson's lyrics were about the seamy side of life: "His world of blues had bad liquor, wild women, and men mistreating women and was tinged with sexuality."[61] Oakley claims Jefferson's expressive lyrics like these from "Lonesome Blues" helped make his songs popular: "I got the blues so bad, it hurts my feet to walk; I got the blues so bad, it hurts my feet to walk; It have settled on my brain and it hurts my tongue to talk."[62]

Most classic blues songs were about romance, but Jefferson and his fellow bluesmen commented on many different topics. Music historian Eileen Southern wrote that they "sang of themselves, of their personal problems, and of their experiences. [Some] songs were mournful laments, others lively dance tunes that set the feet to stomping and seemed to go on forever."[63] Many blues tunes were about how hard it was to be black because of the racism African Americans faced in their daily lives.

The Pain of Black Life

Because racism made life so difficult for southern blacks in the first half of the twentieth century, Jim Crow and economic and social discrimination became the subject of many blues songs. One tune asked this question about whites: "They say we are the Lord's children, I don't say that ain't true; But if we are the same like each other, Ooh, well, well, why do they treat me like they do?"[64] One of the most frightening aspects of black life was a racist justice system that imprisoned blacks falsely or for minor offenses. In "High Sheriff Blues," Charley Patton complained that white sheriffs were always eager to arrest blacks: "Get in trouble at Belzoni [Mississippi], there ain't no use a-screamin' and cryin'; Mister [the law] will take you back to Belzoni jail house flyin'."[65]

Patton was born in Edwards, Mississippi, on April 28, 1891. He is considered the father of Delta blues, a style of country blues that originated in the Delta, the rich agricultural area that cuts through Mississippi and neighboring states. Delta blues had more complex rhythms, longer melodies, and a heavy emphasis on slide guitar techniques. Although Patton's father was illiterate, he owned a general store and lumber-hauling business. Blues historian David Evans claims Patton chose music over business because whites "driven by rampant racism, assigned an inferior caste role to all people of African ancestry. [Charley Patton] wanted a greater degree of freedom than his father had."[66] Patton found that freedom in the blues and in moving north to record songs.

Racism's brutal effect on blacks was evident in 1927 when the Mississippi River flooded southern states like Mississippi, destroying more than 162,000 dwellings and leaving about six hundred thousand people homeless. The black population suffered much greater losses and received less relief than the white population did. Blues singers rushed to record songs about one of the greatest natural disasters ever to hit the South. Blind Lemon described the misery the flood caused when he sang, "Water in Arkansas, people screaming in Tennessee" and "Children stand there screaming: mama we ain't got no home, Oh mama we ain't got no home."[67]

The 1927 Mississippi River flood displaced six hundred thousand people from their homes. The black population suffered disproportionately to whites and blues songwriters wrote songs reflecting on the racism and anguish suffered by black river dwellers.

White officials in charge of disaster relief treated blacks despicably. Whites were allowed to flee the flooding river, but black men, women, and children were forced to work as laborers, sometimes at the point of a gun, to stop the flooding. Blacks toiled ceaselessly to fill bags with dirt and sand and pile them along the Mississippi in a vain attempt to hold back the raging river even as it kept rising dangerously high. As a result, more than 90 percent of the people who drowned in the flood were black; estimates of the dead range from 250 to 1,000. One black convict was shot to death when he complained that whites were making an elderly

The Blues Come to Wisconsin

As strange as it may seem, one of the most prominent early blues recording companies was located in Grafton, Wisconsin, a small community north of Milwaukee whose residents had rarely seen African Americans. Paramount Records was a subsidiary of the Wisconsin Chair Company, which wanted to sell records along with the phonographs it had begun making. In July 1922 Alberta Hunter's "Down Hearted Blues" became the company's first blues record. Paramount recorded singers in Chicago and New York City until 1930, when it set up its Grafton studio. That year Son House and Charley Patton traveled from Mississippi to Grafton to record some songs. In a book about Paramount Records, author Alex van der Tuuk quoted House discussing how the company treated the singers: "There was a two-story hotel special for all the recorders and when you got there you get your key to your room and [company officials would] take you all around and show you [the town]."[1] Despite the warm reception from company executives, Grafton resident John Grams admitted the African Americans were an unusual sight that sometimes surprised townspeople: "When the artists arrived from Milwaukee with the interurban or streetcar and they got off, the kids would run. They had never seen black people."[2] Yet the small firm in all-white Grafton was an important company in helping popularize the blues in the 1920s and 1930s.

1. Quoted in Alex van der Tuuk. *Paramount's Rise and Fall: A History of the Wisconsin Chair Company and Its Recording Activities.* Denver: Mainspring, 2003, p. 26.

2. Quoted in van der Tuuk. *Paramount's Rise and Fall*, p. 28.

black woman carry large sacks of dirt. Camps that opened for flood victims were segregated, with blacks getting poorer, smaller quarters than whites and worse food. And donated toys were distributed only to white children.

Racism was weaker outside the South, but blacks still faced discrimination in housing and jobs. For example, blacks were allowed to live in only the poorest parts of big cities. And although blacks could get better jobs than they could in the South, they were usually paid less than whites and often limited to the hardest, most demeaning jobs available. The racism that allowed lower pay for blacks was one reason music companies began recording men instead of women. Historian Angela Y. Davis claims one reason record companies turned to male singers is that they could pay them less than female singers, who made good money singing in cabarets and tent shows. Davis writes that black bluesmen "were sought out aggressively by profit-hungry recording companies that paid them paltry sums [sometimes just five dollars a song] for their recorded performances."[68] Davis notes that some companies are still selling those recordings on CDs today.

The continued discrimination blacks faced outside the South combined with a sense of alienation in their new surroundings to make many transplanted blacks feel homesick. Blues singers commented about the longing blacks living in Chicago and Detroit had for their old homes. One song claimed, "I'm goin' back South if I wear out ninety-nine pair o' shoes; Then I know I'll be welcome n' I wont have the stranger's blues."[69]

Robert and the Devil

Some bluesmen never left the South, like Robert Johnson, the most legendary of all country blues singers. Blues historian Giles Oakley writes, "The legend of Robert Johnson has been created from the combination of the tragic brevity of his life and the overwhelming sense of inner torment and foreboding in his blues."[70] Born on May 8, 1911, in Hazlehurst, Mississippi, Johnson died on August 16, 1938, at age twenty-seven. As a child, Johnson was shuffled between several homes after a racist mob forced his foster father to leave town because he had dared to argue with a white landowner over a business matter. In 1929 Johnson, a laborer on a plantation near Robinsonville, Mississippi, married sixteen-year-old Virginia Travis; in April 1930 his wife died while giving birth to their child. Johnson began playing the guitar after his wife's death. He tried to learn to play by watching country blues greats like Charley Patton and Son House when they performed near Robinsonville. House, who called the small, slender

Blues singer-songwriter and guitarist Robert Johnson, left, with his partner Johnny Shines in 1935. Johnson only recorded a couple of dozen songs before his death at twenty-seven from poisoning.

Robert Johnson Returns

When Robert Johnson returned to Robinsonville, Mississippi, in the mid-1930s after several years in Hazlehurst, Mississippi, even blues great Son House was amazed at how well he played. House describes the first time he and fellow blues guitarist Willie Brown heard Johnson play:

> Willie and I were playing out at a little place east of Robinsonville called Banks, Mississippi. We were playing there one Saturday night, and all of a sudden somebody came in through the door. Who but him! He had a guitar swinging on his back. I said, "Bill!" He said, "Huh?" I said, "Look who's coming in the door." He looked and said, "Yeah. Little Robert." I said, "And he's got a guitar." And Willie and I laughed about it. Robert finally wiggled through the crowd and got to where we were. He spoke, and I said, "Well, boy, you still got a guitar, huh? What do you do with that thing? You can't do nothing with it." He said, "Well, I'll tell you what." I said, "What?" He said, "Let me have your seat a minute." So I said, "All right, and you better do something with it, too," and I winked my eye at Willie. So he sat down there and finally got started. And man! He was so good! When he finished, all our mouths were standing open. I said, "Well, ain't that fast! He's gone now."

Quoted in Samuel Charters. "Seeking the Greatest Bluesman." *American Heritage*, July–August, 1991, p. 50.

Johnson "Little Robert," claims the neophyte guitarist was lousy at first: "He'd sit at our feet and play during the breaks and such a racket you never heard."[71] Johnson moved back home to Hazlehurst for about a year, and when he returned to Robinsonville, he could play better than anyone else. Johnny Shines, a blues guitarist and good friend of Johnson's, described how much Johnson's musical talent had grown while he was away: "His guitar seemed to talk—repeat and say words with him like no one else in the world could. I said he had a talking guitar, and many a person agreed with me."[72] The ability to make his guitar "talk" was a reference to a traditional blues technique in which players use a slide to manipulate guitar strings and produce high-pitched tones that emulate human speech.

His new skill came from a musical apprenticeship he served with Ike Zinermon, a talented Hazlehurst guitarist. However, a song Johnson wrote called "Me and the Devil Blues" ignited the myth that he gained his guitar wizardry by making a deal with the devil. The song does not mention a bargain with Satan, but references to the devil and hell in several of Johnson's songs led people to believe he had sold his soul for his new talent.

Johnson rambled from town to town, playing on street corners and at dances and juke joints, or rowdy black bars. He eventually came to the attention of record producers at Vocalion Records. In November 1936 the record company brought him to San Antonio, Texas, to record several songs, including "Kind Hearted Woman Blues" and "Terraplane Blues"; Terraplane was the name of a car from that period. In a second recording session in Dallas in 1937, Johnson recorded other songs, including "Hellhound." Paid small sums of money for his work, Johnson went back to playing wherever someone would hire him.

On August 13, 1938, when Johnson was performing at a club called Three Forks just outside of Itta Bena, Mississippi, someone handed him a bottle of whiskey and he drank from it. Johnson quickly became ill and had to quit playing. When Johnson died three days later, people claimed he had been a victim of an "ice curse"—whiskey treated with poison. The culprit was never found, but many assume that a jealous lover or someone jealous that Johnson was romancing his wife or girlfriend poisoned him.

Passing on the Blues

The tragedy of Johnson's early death is that he only recorded about two dozen songs, far fewer than many of his contemporaries. Johnson's death at a young age was reminiscent of that of Lemon Jefferson, who was thirty-six when he died in Chicago in December 1929. The cause of Jefferson's death is not known. Jefferson was found dead outside during the winter, and theories about what killed him include a heart attack, freezing to death from the cold, or even being poisoned by a jealous lover like Johnson.

One of the many copies of Jefferson's records at the B.B. King Museum in Indianola, Mississippi. Jefferson's blues legacy continued after his tragic death in 1929.

The two country blues greats, however, had more in common than dying young under mysterious circumstances. Son House once explained why Johnson's guitar playing sounded so much like that of Blind Lemon: "How it come that he played Lemon's style is this—little Robert learnt from me, and I learnt from an old fellow they call Lemon down in Clarksdale, and he was called Lemon because he had learnt all Blind Lemon's pieces off the phonograph."[73]

The fact that Johnson sounded like Blind Lemon a decade after he died is not uncommon in the blues. Blues singers and instrumentalists have a long tradition of borrowing from each other, everything from how someone plays the guitar to the topics of songs. That tradition has helped the blues evolve from the first primitive forms of the music to the type of music people love today.

Chapter Four

The Blues Move North

When the Great Depression began in 1929, several recording companies went out of business, and others drastically reduced the number of records they released because so few people had money to buy them. The Depression also marked the end of the classic blues era because it was cheaper to record male country blues stars than female singers backed by small bands. As a result, women were never again as dominant in the blues as they were during the 1920s. The end of the decade, however, saw the rise of one of the most influential female blues singers of all time—Memphis Minnie, one of the few women who was ever the equal of male country blues stars.

Memphis Minnie was born Lizzie Douglas on June 3, 1897, in Algiers, Louisiana. In 1929, when Douglas began recording, a record company executive changed her stage name to "Memphis," because Douglas had performed there for many years, and "Minnie," because of the popularity of Mickey Mouse's girlfriend, Minnie. Unlike classic blues singers, Minnie accompanied herself on the guitar. Blues historian Tony Russell writes that she was as good a player as she was a singer: "She was the only female blues artist who matched her male contemporaries as both a singer and an instrumentalist. According to 'Big Bill'

Broonzy, whom Memphis Minnie once beat in a blues battle, she could 'Pick a guitar as good as any man . . . make a guitar cry, moan, talk and whistle the blues.'"[74]

That blues sing-off took place in Chicago, where Memphis Minnie and William "Big Bill" Broonzy had both moved from the South to escape racism. In the 1930s and 1940s, they would be joined by many other blues singers and musicians as the Great Migration that began during World War I continued. Minnie and Broonzy were also involved in the stylistic changes the blues underwent during this period. Both singers switched from acoustic to electric guitar, and Broonzy added other in-strumentalists to his performances as he helped create a new style called urban blues. During this creative period in musical history, the blues also helped spawn new types of black music like boogie-woogie and spirituals. The city most responsible for these new styles was Chicago, a favored destination of southern blacks.

The Migration Continues

William Broonzy, whose parents had both been slaves, was born on June 26, 1893, in Scott, Mississippi. He is an example of why so many blacks were fleeing the South. After serving with the U.S. Army in France during the war, Broonzy returned home in 1919 expecting whites to treat him with more respect for having fought for his country. He once said, "In the army, I had been used to be-ing considered a man [regardless of skin color]."[75] Instead, whites Broonzy met still used racial slurs and made it clear he would never be treated as their equal.

The racism he still encountered motivated Broonzy to move to Chicago a year later. If Broonzy had stayed in the South, his desire for equality might have ended with him being lynched. Lynch-ing was a tactic used frequently in the South to punish blacks for almost any offense against the whites' rules and social restrictions. Tuskegee Institute records show that between 1882 and 1968, rac-ist whites lynched at least 3,445 African American men, women, and children. A lynching occurs when a group of people murder someone by hanging, shooting, burning, or beating him or her to death, and many blacks were lynched because they fought racism and demanded their rights.

Memphis Minnie

Lizzie "Memphis Minnie" Douglas was one of the first women to play an electric guitar. Although her electric blues were never recorded, celebrated African American poet Langston Hughes wrote about an electric blues performance she gave on December 31, 1942:

> The electric guitar is very loud, science having magnified all its softness away. . . . Minnie's feet in high-heeled shoes keep time to the music of her electric guitar. Her thin legs move like musical pistons. . . . She grabs the microphone and yells, "Hey, now!" Then she hits a few deep chords at random, leans forward ever so slightly over her guitar, bows her head, and begins to beat out a good old steady down-home rhythm on the strings—a rhythm so contagious that often it makes the crowd holler out loud. Then Minnie smiles. Her gold teeth flash for a split second. Her earrings tremble. Her left hand with dark red nails move up and down the strings on the guitar's neck. Her right hand with the dice ring on

> it picks out the tune, throbs out the rhythm, beats out the blues. . . . [Her playing blasted out of] the amplifiers like Negro heartbeats mixed with iron and steel. The way Memphis Minnie swings, it sometimes makes folk snap their fingers, women get up and move their bodies, men holler, "Yes!" When they do Minnie smiles.

Langston Hughes. "Here to Yonder." *Chicago Defender*, January 9, 1943. www.hobemianrecords .com/memphisminniehomepage.html.

Memphis Minnie, shown here with an acoustic guitar, was one of the first women to play an electric guitar.

Hanging was the preferred lynching method. In 1939 blues great Billie Holiday sang "Strange Fruit," a song whose title poetically conveyed the brutal image of black bodies hanging from southern trees. Even though Holiday had grown up in the North and never witnessed a lynching, she felt deeply about the need to condemn the racist practice: "I worked like the devil on it, because I was never sure I could put it across or that I could get across to a plush nightclub audience the things that it meant to me."[76]

African Americans living in the North were safer from violence and usually had better jobs and living conditions than southern blacks. However, northern blacks faced racism in their daily lives, including job discrimination; some companies refused to hire blacks, and most companies paid them less money for doing the same jobs as whites. Like other blues musicians, Broonzy had to work regular jobs to supplement the small amounts he received for making records and performing. In "Black, Brown and White," Broonzy summed up this discrimination by singing:

If you're black and gotta work for a living,

This is what they will say to you,

They says, "If you was white, should be all right,

If you was brown, stick around,

But as you's black, hmm brother, get back, get back, get back."[77]

African Americans had more trouble finding work during the Depression because white-owned companies usually hired whites for the few jobs that were available. A communal African American solution to such discrimination was the rent party, in which people who needed cash charged others admission to parties that featured food, drink, and music. Blues musicians sometimes made as little as twenty-five cents for performing at the parties. But pianist James P. Johnson said blues musicians loved the parties because they could eat and drink as much as they wanted: "[You] went from one party to another and everybody made a fuss about you and fed you ice cream, cake, food and drinks. In fact, some of the biggest men in the profession were known as the biggest eaters

William "Big Bill" Broonzy was the son of slaves. Fed up with the racism in the south, Broonzy moved to Chicago in 1920. More black musicians would follow Broonzy to the North.

we had. At an all-night party, you started at 1 A.M., had another meal at 4 A.M."[78]

As black populations continued to grow in northern cities, clubs opened that featured blues music, which gave more blacks the opportunity to earn a living playing and singing. These clubs also helped the blues evolve because they exposed musicians and singers to new ideas from their fellow bluesmen and blueswomen.

The Urban Blues

During the 1930s the blues took root in northern cities like Detroit, Indianapolis, Kansas City, and St. Louis. Chicago became the northern blues capitol because it was the only city in which music companies continued to record the blues. Thomas A. "Georgia Tom" Dorsey moved to Chicago from Atlanta in early 1917. Dorsey said that as the number of black musicians grew, they began to meet each other more often and discuss music: "The House of Jazz Music Store was a hangout for jazz musicians and showfolks. I would go into the store now and then just to have some place to go and be around musicians."[79]

The name of the store shows that even a blues piano player like Dorsey was being influenced by other musical styles. And because most blacks who bought records and came to nightclubs

Big Bill and the Urban Blues

William "Big Bill" Broonzy helped popularize the urban blues in Chicago after moving there as a country blues singer. Blues historian Arnold Shaw explains how Broonzy's style changed during the period in which the new blues was born:

> The transformation of Big Bill's performing style came about largely as a result of two bluesmen, pop-oriented Leroy Carr and jazz-oriented Lonnie Johnson. His efforts at imitating them in his dime-store [record] releases began attracting a public that no longer responded to cryin' country blues. "Young people say you're cryin' when you sing," he later said. "Who wants to cry? Well, back in the early days, what else could black people and bluesmen do but cry? Having stopped crying, Broonzy proceeded to develop a pleasant, ingratiating style of delivery, evident in [records] he made after 1934. The change was apparent in the optimistic "The Sun Gonna Shine in My Back Door Some Day." . . . The years from 1936 to 1939 were peak recording years for Big Bill [and] saw him move from a piano-accompanied bluesman to one for whom rhythmic punch became vital. . . . By 1939 he was recording with a combo called Big Bill & His Memphis Five consisting of trumpet, alto sax, string bass, guitar, and piano.

Arnold Shaw. *Honkers and Shouters: The Golden Years of Rhythm & Blues.* New York: Macmillan, 1978, p. 24.

to hear the blues had similar wide-ranging musical tastes, a new urban blues sound emerged. This new blues was more sophisticated and up-tempo than country blues. Singers began to have bigger backup groups with musicians playing piano, drums, harmonica, and even wind instruments like the saxophone. Blues historian Robert Santelli explains the new music's appeal: "[The] sound seemed hotter and more exciting than the sound generated by a singer and a single acoustic guitar."[80] In the late 1930s and early 1940s, blues musicians started playing electric guitars with amplifiers.

The new style changed how blues musicians played guitar, still the dominant blues instrument. Lonnie Johnson was a country blues singer who successfully made the transition to urban blues. Johnson was credited with being a creative player who incorporated jazz and other popular music styles into his guitar playing that made his music more sophisticated and expressive. Blues historian David R. Adler claims, "He was there to help define the instrument's future within [the blues and] his melodic conceptions were so far advanced from most of his peers as to inhabit a plane all his own."[81]

The urban blues also dealt with different subject matter than country blues. Blacks living in big northern cities had different experiences than blacks in the rural South. Although many songs still focused on love relationships and the problems of daily life, many urban blues tunes were more upbeat about the future. An example is a song Broonzy wrote and sang titled "Just a Dream." The lyrics include, "Dreamed I was in the White House, sittin' in the president's chair; I dreamed he's shaking my hand, and he said 'Bill, I'm so glad you're here.'"[82] Urban blues songs also talked about African American accomplishments. In 1938 Bill Gaither's "Champ Joe Louis" celebrated black heavyweight boxing champion Joe Louis's victory over German boxing champion Max Schmeling. The song's lyrics boasted, "It was only two minutes and four seconds, poor Schmeling was down on his knee; He looked like he was praying to the Good Lord to 'Have mercy on me, please!'"[83] African Americans gloried in Louis's ring triumphs.

Urban blues songs also began to scrap the traditional blues structures like the AAB formula for lyrics. An example is the 1928 song "How Long, How Long Blues" by Leroy Carr, one of

Lonnie Johnson was a jazz and country blues singer-guitarist who incorporated jazz and other popular music styles into his playing.

the earliest urban blues tunes. Carr, who was born in Nashville, Tennessee, and grew up in Indianapolis, teamed with guitarist Francis "Scrapper" Blackwell on that historic song. The song's verses are eight bars long instead of twelve as in earlier blues, and Carr never repeats the first line of any of them. The song was so popular that blues historian Francis Davis wrote, "We owe the very concept of the urban blues to Carr and Blackwell [because its commercial success] sent record company representatives in search of talent in cities, not just in rural outposts."[84] In cities like Indianapolis, where Carr resided, other new types of blues were soon discovered.

Other Blues Variations

During the 1930s a piano-based blues called boogie-woogie became popular in cities like Chicago and Kansas City. A mainstay at rent parties because it was fun to dance to, the new style featured blues guitar techniques adapted for piano. In 1935 Clarence "Pinetop" Smith was the first to record a song with the new name in the title—"Pinetop's Boogie Woogie." The song's lyrics included these dance instructions: "Brand new number, folks, called Boogie Woogie!; It's a funny little song. Now, when I tell you to hold it, I don't want you to move a thing; And when I tell you to get it, I want you to Boogie Woogie!"[85] The song's infectious, joyful beats helped boogie-woogie become so popular that it spread to big bands, the jazz-oriented orchestras with twelve to twenty-five musicians that were popular at the time. Such bands led by William "Count" Basie and other black musicians performed blues songs as well as jazz and popular tunes.

Hokum was another new blues style. It began in 1928 when guitarist Hudson "Tampa Red" Whittaker and Georgia Tom Dorsey recorded "It's Tight like That," a humorous song filled with sexual innuendoes. Dorsey explained years later how he and Tampa Red came up with the name *hokum*: "We didn't want to call ourselves blues singers, and we didn't want to call ourselves popular singers. I don't know what 'hokum' means [but] it was a good word to carry, for nobody knew what it meant."[86] The two musicians performed for a while as the Hokum Boys. The craze was short-lived, but the style is considered a forerunner of songs today that praise wild party behavior.

Blacks in different areas of the nation also began developing regional styles like the West Coast blues, songs that are dominated by strong piano playing and guitar solos with a jazz influence. But even as blacks were creating different or subtle variations of blues, the blues began to influence white musical composers. George Gershwin's *Rhapsody in Blue* in 1924 was heavily influenced by both jazz and the blues, and his 1935 opera *Porgy and Bess* about blacks living in the South was even more blues oriented. Black music historian Earl L. Stewart writes: "White composers like Irving Berlin, George Gershwin, and Jerome Kern were obviously aware of blues elements and often incorporated them into their music. The craze for 'blues' type songs in the 1920s and 1930s led many popular composers to [put blues] elements into their compositions."[87]

In addition to such formal white music, the blues also helped shape the creation of country music. One of the earliest country stars in the 1920s was Jimmie Rodgers, who learned to love the blues while growing up in Mississippi. Hailed by many as the "Father of Country Music," Rodgers became famous by writing early country songs that were strongly influenced by the blues. Rodgers also recorded blues tunes like "Long Tall Mama Blues" and "T.B. Blues." The latter song about tuberculosis, a deadly disease that killed thousands of people in the early twentieth century, included the lyrics, "I've been fightin' like a lion, looks like I'm going to lose, I've been fightin' like a lion looks like I'm going to lose, 'Cause there ain't nobody ever whipped the TB blues, I've got the TB blues."[88] Rodgers had tuberculosis when he wrote and

Country singer Jimmie Rodgers is hailed by many as the "Father of Country Music." Strongly influenced by the blues, Rodgers would record many blues tunes, even yodeling the blues in some.

sang the song in 1932, and he died from the disease on May 26, 1933. The Carter Family, one of the most storied groups in country music, also sang blues songs early in their career.

The blues was also an inspiration for another new type of music in the 1930s. Surprisingly, it was a new genre of sacred music—gospel. Like black spirituals, gospel is based on Christianity and a love of God, but it is more joyous than black spirituals. Gospel music was influenced by both the blues and jazz.

Gospel and Blues: Sacred and Profane

Even though blues songs usually center on base themes like fighting, sex, and drinking, there has always been a strong connection between them and sacred music. First, it must be remembered that spirituals, religious songs blacks sang in the nineteenth century, were one of the earlier African American musical styles that shaped the blues. Secondly, most blues musicians were familiar with religious songs from attending church when they were young. Blues historian William Ferris writes, "Blues and sacred music are joined at the hip. [One] blues musician told me that if a singer wants to cross over from sacred music to the blues, he simply replaces 'my God' with 'my baby' and continued singing the same song."[89]

Many blues musicians had a strong emotional attachment to religious music because most of them grew up listening to it as children. Thus, it is not as strange as it might seem that one of the originators of gospel music was blues musician Georgia Tom Dorsey. Dorsey grew up in Georgia, where his father was a minister. Dorsey studied music formally in Chicago. He played piano for Gertrude "Ma" Rainey and with Tampa Red before turning to gospel full-time. Dorsey explained once why his Gospel music had blues overtones: "Blues is a part of me, the way I play the piano, the way I write."[90] In 1932 Dorsey's wife died giving birth to their son, who died two days later. The tragedy inspired Dorsey to write "Precious Lord, Take My Hand," arguably one of the greatest of all gospel songs.

Although Dorsey had written some gospel music before that, the family tragedy led him to give up writing and singing blues music completely. Some blues stars like "Sister" Rosetta Tharpe and Ida Goodson had successful careers singing both gospel and

Blues musician and an originator of gospel music, Thomas A. "Georgia Tom" Dorsey poses with his renown female gospel quartet in 1934. He played piano for Ma Rainey and Tampa Red Whittaker.

the blues, even though the blues was sometimes referred to as "the devil's music." As Goodson once explained, "the Devil got his work and God got his work"[91] from her because she sang both types of music. Other blues singers and musicians abandoned church music once they began playing the blues. Country blues

Billie Holiday

Billie Holiday did not have to endure the brutal racism blacks experienced in southern states, because she grew up in Philadelphia and New York City. But like other black entertainers, the singer known as Lady Day for the elegance of her performances was not exempt from racist treatment. In 1938 Holiday broke a racial barrier as the first black singer with a major band. When the Artie Shaw Band performed at New York's Lincoln Hotel, Holiday had to use the Service Entrance while white performers entered through the hotel's front door. Once in St. Louis, Missouri, the white club owner who hired the band to play asked "What's that n----- doing there: I don't [even] have n------ to clean up around here."[1] Holiday also wrote about how racism affected her when the band traveled to segregated areas in the South:

> Sometimes we'd make a six-hundred mile jump and stop only
> once. Then it would be a place where I couldn't get served let
> alone [use] the toilet without causing a scene. At first I used to be
> ashamed. Then finally I just said to hell with it. When I had to go
> I'd just ask the bus driver to stop and let me off at the side of the
> road. I'd rather go in the bushes than take a chance in the restau-
> rants and towns.[2]

1. Quoted in Angela Y. Davis. *Blues Legacies and Black Feminism: Gertrude "Ma" Rainey, Bessie Smith, and Billie Holiday.* New York: Pantheon, 1998, p. 49.

2. Quoted in Davis. *Blues Legacies and Black Feminism*, p. 193.

In 1938 the incomparable blues singer Billie Holiday became the first black singer to play with a major band—the Artie Shaw Band. When traveling with the white band she had to endure racism and segregation from New York to the Deep South.

star Eddie "Son" House was born in Riverton, Mississippi, on March 21, 1902. By age fifteen House had realized his childhood dream of being a Baptist preacher, but his love of the blues and his wild temper—he served two years in prison for killing a man in a fight—eventually led him away from preaching and religious music.

Not long after leaving prison in 1930, House recorded "Preachin' the Blues," a song that described his inner torment because he loved both the church and the blues. The song's lyrics include, "Oh in my room I bowed down to pray; Oh I was in my room I bowed down to pray; Say the blues come 'long and they drove my spirit [love of God] away."[92]

Theologian James Cone, who is African American, believes the blues and spiritual songs are bound together by more than musical similarities. He claims that blues songs are really secular spirituals because they attempt to express the same ideas and feelings as religious songs. Cone writes: "They [blues songs] are secular in . . . that they confine their attention solely to the immediate and affirm the bodily expression of black soul, including its sexual manifestations. They are spirituals because they are impelled by the same search for the truth of black experience."[93]

Chapter Five

The Blues Evolve

The April 19, 1937, issue of *Life* magazine included a story with a headline that would be considered racist today—"Bad N----- Makes Good Minstrel." The article was about Huddie "Lead Belly" Ledbetter. One photograph accompanying the text was a close-up of his hands on the neck of his guitar—the caption beneath it read, "These hands once killed a man." The article noted, with a tone of amazement, that Lead Belly was a stage and radio blues star even though he had twice been sentenced to thirty-year prison terms for brutal crimes—in 1917 for murder in Texas and in 1930 for assault with intent to commit murder for beating a white man in Louisiana. The story's condescending tone claimed:

> The easiest way to avoid or at least to mitigate the consequences of sin is to entertain your fellow man. Amuse the public, and you can get away with almost any crime. [Twice] imprisoned for murder or attempted murder, he has twice strummed and sung his way to gubernatorial pardons, is celebrated today as the country's No. 1 Negro minstrel.[94]

Both times Lead Belly was incarcerated, he endeared himself to guards and officials with his music; Texas governor Pat M. Neff invited friends to prison on Sundays to hear his star prisoner play. Both times Lead Belly was imprisoned, he served only a few years because governors freed him after hearing songs he wrote seeking a pardon. Lead Belly's second bid for freedom was backed by John Lomax, who recorded him when he was a Texas prisoner in 1933 for a Library of Congress collection of African American music. After being released a second time, Lead Belly became a blues star.

Huddie "Lead Belly" Ledbetter was an ex-convict who started playing blues guitar and writing with Blind Lemon in 1915. He was the last of the great country blues singers.

When Lead Belly died in New York City on December 6, 1949, at age sixty, one music historian claimed it meant "the traditional blues as a living, creative force had come to an end."[95] In one way that statement was correct. Lead Belly, who in 1915 had traveled with "Blind" Lemon Jefferson and learned some of his guitar techniques, was perhaps the last great country blues singer. However, a host of creative musicians would continue to help the blues evolve from the tradition of a lone singer strumming a guitar.

The Modern Blues

One of those historic blues innovators was McKinley "Muddy Waters" Morganfield, who once claimed, "I took the old-time music and brought it up to date."[96] In the late 1940s Muddy was the prime creator of modern Chicago blues, an electrified, amplified version of the country blues he learned to love while growing up in Mississippi. Born on April 4, 1913, in Jug's Corner, Morganfield won his nickname as a child for playing in and even eating mud. He had little formal schooling and began doing agricultural work like picking cotton when he was eight. At age fourteen, Muddy heard country blues great Son House, fell in love with the blues, and was soon performing locally.

On August 31, 1941, Muddy met Alan Lomax on the Stovall plantation where he worked. Like his father, John, who had discovered Lead Belly, Lomax was preserving black music for the Library of Congress. Muddy was stunned that a white man wanted to record him but sang "I's Be Troubled," a song he had written three years earlier. Its lyrics included, "Well if I feel tomorrow, like I feel today; I'm gonna pack my suitcase, and make my getaway; Lord I'm troubled, I'm all worried in mind; And I'm never bein' satisfied, and I just can't keep from cryin'."[97] Lomax later wrote, "I realized I had recorded a masterpiece."[98] The recording session was even more important to Muddy because he said it made him believe he had a future as a blues singer: "I sounded just like anybody's records. Man, you don't know how I felt that afternoon when I heard that voice and it was my own voice. I thought, 'Man, I can sing.' Later on he sent me two copies of the pressing and [I] just played it and played it and said, 'I can do it, I can do it.'"[99]

Muddy moved to Chicago in 1943 to pursue that dream, working day jobs while playing the blues at night at parties and

McKinley "Muddy Waters" Morganfield played electric guitar and modernized the blues, but kept the songs true to the lyric traditions of country blues greats.

in clubs. Muddy's big break came in April 1948 with his first hit record, "I Can't Be Satisfied," an updated version of the song he sang for Lomax. When the first three thousand copies of the record sold out overnight, Muddy was on his way to becoming a star. The new sound Muddy popularized was one he had honed in Chicago nightclubs, which were so noisy that he had switched to electric guitar and added other backup musicians. This is how Muddy described the new blues:

> [You] get more of a pure thing out of an acoustic, but you get more noise out of an amplifier. If you get the piano in there you get a whole full bed of background music. I kept that backbeat on the drums plus full action on the guitar and [electric] harmonica. Then you've got a big sound. It was in my head. Nobody ever told me about it.[100]

Despite modernizing the blues, Muddy kept the songs true to the lyrical traditions of country blues greats Son House and Robert Johnson. But other musicians even more willing to scrap tradition began adding new tempos and rhythms to the blues to create new types of music.

Rhythm and Blues

Billboard is a weekly magazine that since the 1930s has published lists of the nation's most popular songs. In its June 25, 1949, issue, *Billboard* scrapped the "Race" title for black music that had been used since 1920 when the first blues records were released. The new heading, "Rhythm and Blues," often shortened to R&B, included blues and other new black music. One reason for the change was that the old title seemed bigoted and crude. The new name also reflected the wider range of music African Americans were now playing. Blues historian Robert Santelli explains why the blues began to change in that era: "The story of the blues in the 1940s is the story of a people and a music on the move. [For] the blues to remain an important part of black culture, it had to absorb new ideas, new sounds, new ways of delivering the emotional highs and lows of black country folk in the city. And that's exactly what happened."[101]

Musical changes included the songs of bluesmen like Muddy Waters, Chester "Howlin' Wolf" Burnett, and B.B. King who fought to preserve the basic essence of the blues while updating its sound. But some new types of blues-based music seemed far removed from traditional blues—its lyrics were happier and more positive than the often gloomy older songs and it had more complex and often lighter, bouncier beats and melodies. King claims the new blues reflected the happier mood of African Americans in

Louis Jordan

Louis Jordan's innovative music helped create the rhythm-and-blues style of music and influenced the sound of some early rock-and-roll groups like Bill Haley and His Comets. Jordan was one of the 1940s' most popular bandleaders, and many of his fans were white. Jordan once discussed his success in attracting white fans with blues historian Arnold Shaw:

> After my records started to sell, we drew mixed audiences to clubs [in cities around the nation]. The first time I played the Adams Theatre in Newark, I played with a fellow who sings like [white singer] Perry Como [and] the second time I played there, I appeared with a society band like Meyer Davis. I was the Negro part, and they played the white part. That's how we did it in the early forties, so that we drew everybody. I was trying to do what they told me: straddle the fence. I made just as much money off white people as I did off colored. Any time I played a white theater, my black following was there [but] many nights we had more white than colored, because my records were geared to the white as well as colored, and they came to hear me do my records.

Quoted in Arnold Shaw. *Honkers and Shouters: The Golden Years of Rhythm & Blues*. New York: Macmillan, 1978, pp. 67–68.

Louis Jordan, on saxophone, jams onstage with his band the Tympany Five. Jordan's innovations spawned the rhythm-and-blues style of music and influenced many early rock-and-roll groups.

this period. America's entry into World War II in 1941 had creat-ed a second wave of black migration out of the South, and by the time the fighting ended in 1945, the nation's robust economy had improved general living standards for most blacks. King claims even poor Mississippi blacks were happier. "We could feel the optimism of post-war America," said King, adding, "I could feel optimism in the happy music of Louis Jordan."[102]

Louis Jordan was the biggest star of jump blues, an up-tempo style featuring small bands including a horn section that was pop-ular in the 1940s. Born on July 8, 1908, in Brinkley, Arkansas, Jordan grew up in a musical household—his father taught music and led bands like the Rabbit Foot Minstrels. In 1939 Jordan, who played saxophone, formed the Tympany Five, a combo that in-cluded a guitar, bass, piano, and drums. Jordan had a humorous style, and his goal was to please his audience. He once claimed that jazz musicians "play for themselves [but] I want to play for the people."[103] Jordan succeeded because from 1942 to 1951 he recorded fifty-seven songs that made it to *Billboard*'s list of rhythm-and-blues hits.

The lively tunes and lush musical accompaniment of Jordan's songs provided a playful background for the hilarious lyrics of his hits. When the U.S. government began rationing food dur-ing the war, his "Ration Blues" jokingly began, "Baby baby baby, what's wrong with Uncle Sam?; He's cut down on my sugar, now he's messin' with my ham; Oh me, I've got those ration blues."[104] His songs included whimsical lyrics like these from his million-selling "Choo Choo Ch'Boogie," in which Jordan commented on the hardships of wartime train travel: "Choo-choo, choo-choo, ch'boogie, woo-woo; Woo-woo, ch'boogie, choo-choo, choo-choo, ch'boogie; Take me right back to the track, jack."[105] And his "Let the Good Times Roll" in 1946 became the nation's anthem for postwar gaiety:

> Hey, everybody, let's have some fun,
>
> You only live but once,
>
> And when you're dead you're done, so,
>
> Let the good times roll, let the good times roll,
>
> I don't care if you're young or old,
>
> Get together, let the good times roll.[106]

Arthur "Big Boy" Crudup was a Mississippian who moved to Chicago in 1940 and played street corners and lived on the streets. He had a string of small hits in the 1940s.

Jordan, more than anyone else, helped create rhythm and blues. Aaron Thibeaux "T-Bone" Walker, one of the 1940s' flashiest electric blues guitar players, once stated, "Jordan plays good blues,"[107] even though he had broken away from classic blues traditions, because he felt Jordan's work retained the essence of blues music. Jordan, however, was only one of many singers and musicians who were experimenting with the blues. In the process, they would all help pave the way for the birth of rock and roll.

Fats Domino

———————◼———————

Rolling Stone magazine once claimed that the only rock-and-roll star more popular during the 1950s than Elvis Presley was Fats Domino. Antoine Dominique "Fats" Domino's lively boogie-woogie blues style piano and pleasant though high-pitched voice made him one of the few African American stars in the early days of rock and roll. Fats Domino had a string of rock hits like "Ain't That a Shame," "I'm Walking," and "Blueberry Hill," a 1956 record that sold more than 5 million copies. Fats was so popular that he appeared in two 1956 rock-and-roll films—*Shake, Rattle and Rock!* and *The Girl Can't Help It*. His concerts, often played to predominantly white audiences, were sellouts. In a February 1957 story, *Ebony* magazine reported that his fans went crazy during his performances: "When Elvis Presley sings, teen-agers swoon and drop for dead. Pat Boone hits them in the limbs and they flop around like headless chickens. But when Fats Domino sings, mass hysteria sets in."[1] In the article Fats commented on his sudden popularity in the new style of music: "I guess it's the beat that they like and some people say there's something in my voice. I don't say that 'cause I haven't got a [great] voice. But the beat, it's something the kids can dance by. . . . There's nothing new about the music. I've been playing it for years as rhythm and blues."[2]

1. *Ebony*. "King of Rock 'n' Roll." February 1957, p. 26.
2. Quoted in *Ebony*. "King of Rock 'n' Roll," p. 26.

Rock-and-Roll Ancestors

Muddy Waters wrote "The Blues Had a Baby and They Called It Rock 'n' Roll," a song that jokingly refers to the direct link between the two musical styles. For example, the small combos Jordan created to play his songs as well as some of his music helped set the pattern for rock-and-roll bands. And many other blues musicians were also important in creating a music phenomenon in the second half of the twentieth century that would quickly sweep its way around the world.

When Arthur "Big Boy" Crudup moved to Chicago from Forest, Mississippi, around 1940, he played for change on street corners and lived in a wooden box under the city's elevated train tracks.

In 1946 he recorded "That's All Right, Mama," an up-tempo blues tune that began "Well, that's all right, mama, That's all right for you; That's all right mama, just anyway you do."[108] Crudup was an average guitarist, and blues historian. Arnold Shaw claims, "For a big man, he had a high-pitched, shrill voice and sang in a style imitative of the hollers of field hands."[109] But the record became one of a string of small hits Crudup had in the 1940s, including "So Glad You're Mine" and "My Baby Left Me."

In New Orleans, Antoine "Fats" Domino was creating fans by playing the piano. A July 1949 New Orleans newspaper article asked readers: "Say Papa have you been to the Hideaway lately. Fats Domino is out there making them holler!!!"[110] Domino—who at 220 pounds (100kg) lived up to his nickname—combined a silky-smooth voice, sparkling piano playing, and catchy lyrics to create hits like "Ain't That a Shame."

T-Bone Walker was as famous for his stage antics as his poetic hit "Call It Stormy Monday," which begins, "They call it stormy Monday, but Tuesday's just as bad [and] Wednesday's worse, and Thursday's also sad."[111] Like country blues star Charley Patton, T-Bone loved doing wild things while playing his guitar; these included the splits and swinging his guitar over his head and strumming its strings. In 1954 Kansas City native "Big" Joe Turner—he was called a blues "shouter" because he sang so lustily—recorded "Shake, Rattle, and Roll." He made the song a hit by lustily screaming out, "I said shake, rattle and roll, shake, rattle and roll; Shake, rattle and roll, shake, rattle and roll; Well, you won't do right to save your doggone soul."[112]

Willie Mae "Big Mama" Thornton—she was 6 feet tall (183cm) and weighed more than 300 pounds (136kg)—was one of the female blues singers who contributed to rock's birth. In her 1953 hit "Hound Dog," Big Mama complained about a wayward lover in her deep, lusty voice by singing, "You ain't nothing but a hound dog, been snoopin' round my door; You can wag your tail, but I ain't gonna feed you no more."[113]

The titles and lyrics of the above tunes are probably familiar to those who love rock and roll, even if they do not know much about the blues. All of those songs were originally blues hits. The fact that they became some of rock's first big hits when they were covered by white singers proves how much rock and roll owes to

T-Bone Walker was famous for his stage antics, including splits and playing the guitar over his head. He recorded the hit "Shake, Rattle, and Roll."

the blues for the themes of its songs, its melodies, and the way performers sing the lyrics.

Rock and Roll Is Born

B.B. King once claimed that "rock 'n' roll was really rhythm and blues performed for white teenagers."[114] In fact, the birth of the new music was inevitable after white teenagers in the late 1940s and early 1950s began listening to black radio stations and buying records by black artists. This phenomenon upset many white adults because blacks and whites in that era rarely socialized. In the 1950s a circular titled "Don't Buy Negro Records," which was distributed in many cities, read, "The screaming idiotic words and savage music of these records are undermining the morals of our white youth in America. Call the advertisers of radio stations that play this type of music and complain to them!"[115]

Racism was partly to blame for that negative attitude. When record companies realized how many white teenagers liked black music, they began recording white singers and musicians playing black hits in order to make the music more acceptable. Blues historian Eileen Southern explains how this phenomenon helped create rock and roll: "[It was a] trend in which a blues or rhythm and blues group relatively unknown (that is, outside black communities) released a best-selling record, white pop singers covered it; and the cover outsold the original, aided by the powerful promotional and distribution facilities of the [white] music industry."[116]

Examples include the 1954 hits Bill Haley and His Comets had when they covered Turner's "Shake, Rattle, and Roll" and Pat Boone's hit when he recorded Domino's "Ain't That a Shame." Rock's biggest early star also owed his initial success to blues-based tunes. Elvis Presley's first hit in 1954 was Crudup's "That's All Right, Mama." Presley also had hits with several other Crudup songs and with Thornton's "Hound Dog." Unaware that a woman had first sung the song, many people wondered why Elvis used a masculine symbol—a hound dog—to refer to his wayward girlfriend.

Presley was born on January 8, 1935, in Tupelo, Mississippi. He grew up listening to the blues and freely admitted that blues singers had influenced him. He once said, "I dug the real low-down Mississippi singers, mostly Big Bill Broonzy and Big Boy Crudup, although they [his parents] would scold me at home for listening to them."[117] Although Presley's versions of blues songs featured his own style, one that had also been influenced by country music, his records retained a blues feel. Francis Davis is one of many music historians who believe Presley was an authentic blues singer and not a blues pretender: "It isn't enough to say that Elvis treated thousands of white teenagers to their first sugared taste of black music and perhaps gave them an appetite for the real thing. That's not giving him his proper due. He was one of the finest white blues singers."[118]

Domino and several other black singers had hit rock songs in the 1950s. Despite those successes, many blues singers were angry that white singers had stolen their music and were making more money than they ever had because white versions of blues hits were more acceptable to the general public. Broonzy, for one, complained, "You hear Elvis Presley, you hearin' Big Boy

B.B. King

Riley "B.B." King did not have to leave the South to become famous. Born in Indianola, Mississippi, on September 16, 1925, he moved to Memphis in the late 1940s and began playing on radio station WDIA as the Beale Street Blues Boy. Fans shortened the name to" Bee-Bee," and ultimately those initials became his nickname. Although he was influenced by blues greats like Aaron Thibeaux "T-Bone" Walker, King worked hard to develop a unique style in which his guitar seems to talk to his audience. King explained how he did this in his autobiography:

> The single factor that drove me to practice was the sound I heard from the Hawaiian or country-and-western steel pedal guitar. That cry sounded human to me. I wanted to sustain a note like a singer. I wanted to phrase a note like a saxophonist. By bending the strings, by trilling my hand—and I have a big left hand—I could achieve something that approximated a vocal vibrato. I could sustain a note. I wanted to connect my guitar to human emotions. By fooling with the feedback between my amplifier and instrument, I started experimenting with sounds that expressed my feelings, whether happy or sad, bouncy or bluesy. I was looking for ways to let my guitar sing.

B.B. King with David Ritz. *Blues All Around Me: The Autobiography of B.B. King.* New York: Avon, 1996, p. 127.

One of the most influential blues guitarist of all time is B.B. King. King developed a unique style of blues guitar that influenced many white guitarists of the rock era, among them Eric Clapton.

Crudup."[119] B.B. King, however, was more understanding about what happened. In his autobiography, King wrote:

> I hold no grudges. Elvis didn't steal any music from anyone. He just had his own interpretation of the music he'd grown up on. [I've] heard blacks say, "Why couldn't the first big rock star be black, since rock came from black music?" The common sense reason is in the numbers. [Blacks] might invent a new style, but chances are, only the white artist's adaptation of that style will result in mass-market success.[120]

That is a very generous statement, because as rock became king of music, the blues went into a steep decline in popularity.

Chapter Six

The Blues Resurgence

When rock and roll emerged in the mid-1950s, many people believed it was a bizarre musical style loved only by teenagers and that it would quickly fade away. But within a decade the loud, untamed songs many older adults wished they could ban from record stores and radio airwaves became the nation's most dominant music. Rock's growing fan base meant a decline in popularity for other types of music. Ironically, this included the blues, for which rock owed its very existence. Recording companies reduced the number of blues records they released, and attendance fell at blues performances because many white blues fans now listened only to rock music. As a result, blues stars like McKinley "Muddy Waters" Morganfield, Chester "Howlin' Wolf" Burnett, and B.B. King struggled financially. Muddy once explained rock's disastrous effect on the blues: "The rock and roll, this hurt the blues pretty bad. We still hustled around and made it and kept goin', but we were only playin' for black people when rock and roll came along."[121] King said the lack of interest in the blues made him feel the music he had always loved and played was outdated and would never again regain its past popularity: "For a large part of the sixties, I fell between the cracks of fashion. Because I couldn't twist and shout, I was seen as a dinosaur."[122]

In 1960 Ernest "Chubby Checker" Evans created a dance craze with a rock version of "The Twist." It was another example of rock and roll covering a rhythm-and-blues hit—Hank Ballard had introduced the song and the dance a year earlier. But at least this time an African American benefited from rock's growing popularity because Chubby was one of a handful of blacks who made the transition to rock. Other black rockers included Fats Domino, "Little" Richard Penniman, Elias "Bo Diddley" Bates, and Chuck Berry, whose creative guitar playing and flamboyant stage antics were a model that would be copied by scores of future rock stars.

Rock and roll's popularity was so strong by the mid-1960s that the blues seemed ready to fade away like many people had thought—and even hoped—rock would. Then a funny thing happened—the blues started to become more popular than ever.

Many African Americans benefited from rock's growing popularity and brought rhythm and blues to rock. Chuck Berry's creative guitar playing, famed "duck walk," and flamboyant stage antics would influence a generation of rock musicians.

And in a bizarre twist of fate, the blues partly owed their resurgence to some of the most famous stars in rock history.

The British Invasion

The Beatles arrived in New York City in February 1964 to begin their first U.S. tour. During a news conference, a reporter asked the four British rockers what they most wanted to see in the United States. To the astonishment of the assembled media, the band members replied Muddy Waters and Bo Diddley. When reporters did not know them, the Beatles chided their ignorance by saying, "You Americans don't seem to know your most famous citizens."[123] The Beatles had arrived as the world's most popular rock group— a sign of their popularity was that in just two weeks, U.S. fans had bought 2.6 million copies of their latest single, "I Want to Hold Your Hand." The fact that their musical heroes were two bluesmen stunned not only reporters but fans of the Beatles as well.

The Beatles led the British Invasion, the arrival of English rock bands like the Rolling Stones, Yardbirds, and Animals who were more popular in the mid-1960s than any U.S. groups. American fans of the British rockers were surprised to discover that most of them loved the blues and worshipped blues musicians that were somewhat obscure in America. During their first U.S. tour in 1964, the Rolling Stones consented to appear on *Shindig* only after producers of the rock show consented to their demand that Howlin' Wolf sing on the same program. Rolling Stones guitarist Keith Richards grew up listening to blues records, especially those of Muddy Waters. He once aptly stated, "The music got called rock and roll [only] because it had gone white; otherwise it was rhythm and blues."[124] Richards and lead singer Mick Jagger loved Muddy so much that the band named itself after his song "Rollin' Stone Blues," and their first big hit, "(I Can't Get No) Satisfaction," was a cover of Muddy's first hit song, "I Can't Be Satisfied."

English rockers had been exposed to the blues through both records and live performances. William "Big Bill" Broonzy toured Europe in 1951, and Muddy and King soon followed Broonzy overseas. After Muddy toured England in 1958, he boasted, "I drove 'em crazy. I went over there and they went nuts."[125] It was not only contemporary blues greats that excited English rock stars. Eric Clapton, one of the greatest of all rock guitarists, owes

The Rolling Stones, like so many British bands of the era, were heavily influenced by American blues and rhythm and blues music.

his musical career to Robert Johnson, who died nearly a decade before Clapton was born in 1945. Clapton was fifteen when he heard a record of Johnson's blues. He said the record was a turning point in his life: "Up until then I thought I was going to be an art student, then get a job or become a painter. I never thought of music as my vocation."[126] Johnson's country blues led Clapton into music, and naturally his first lead vocal was a cover of Johnson's "Ramblin' on My Mind."

The exalted status that rock stars like Richards and Clapton accorded to blues singers helped ignite an explosion of interest in the blues that would make it more popular than ever before.

The Blues Revival

The blues revival that began in the 1960s was also linked to the civil rights movement, which resulted in the growing pride blacks

A Revitalized Muddy Waters

———————————◼———————————

McKinley "Muddy Waters" Morganfield was one of the main beneficiaries of the new interest in the blues that British rock groups created. In an interview in the late 1970s, Muddy explained why it meant so much to have white rockers praise him:

> Before the Rolling Stones, people over here [the United States] didn't know nothing and didn't *want* to know nothing about me. I was making race records, and I'm gonna tell it to you the way the older people told it to the kids. If they'd buy my records, their parents would say, "What the hell is this? Get this n----- record out of my house!" But then the Rolling Stones and those other groups come over here from England, playing this music, and now, today, the kids buy a record of mine, and they listen to it. [Years ago] some of my gigs, I might have a few [white] kids from the university but if it wasn't some school date I was playing, if it was just in a club in Chicago, it would be maybe one percent, two percent white. I play in places now don't have no black faces in there but our black faces.

Quoted in Robert Palmer. *Deep Blues*. New York: Penguin, 1981, p. 260.

had in their heritage as well as a new interest by whites in African American culture. Many whites wanted to learn more about black music, especially the blues. This interest centered on country blues, which was considered the most authentic and original blues and became known as folk blues. This led to the rediscovery of older bluesmen like Son House, Sam "Lightnin'" Hopkins, and Skip James who had lived in virtual obscurity for decades. House, for example, had made some blues records in the 1930s. By 1943, however, he had given up playing because he could not make enough money. He moved to Rochester, New York, where he worked odd jobs as a railroad porter and grill cook. In 1964 the new interest in blues led promoters of the Newport Folk Festival in Rhode Island to seek out House and ask him to play in the prestigious musical event. House was a hit and began performing and recording again. Blues historian Francis Davis explains why House was suddenly revered after having been ignored for so many years: "By virtue of having survived most of his contemporaries, he became a stand-in for all of them, a living link to the holiest blues tradition [like Robert Johnson]."[127]

The early blues boom ignored modern blues because purists claimed Waters and others had corrupted the blues by electrifying them. That changed when British rockers began praising them. King's white fan base, for example, exploded when the Rolling Stones had him join them on their U.S. tour. King said he realized how much his popularity had grown when he played at Fillmore West, a famed rock venue in San Francisco, California. He had been nervous about his reception before a mostly white audience but was overcome with emotion when he went onstage because, as he explained: "By the time I strapped on Lucille [his nickname for his guitar], every single person in the place was standing up and cheering like crazy. For the first time in my career, I got a standing ovation *before* I played. Couldn't help but cry."[128]

The growing blues craze also benefited John Lee Hooker, a Mississippi native who moved to Detroit in 1943. In 1948 his recording of "Boogie Chillen" led him to leave his factory job and play blues full-time. Hooker had a unique style in which he chanted lyrics while playing in one chord and punctuating the song with violent, amplified blues riffs and thumps on his guitar. "My style come from my stepfather," Hooker said. "The style I'm playing now, that's what he was playing."[129] Hits like "Boom, Boom" made him a star even though he sounded different from singers like King and Wolf.

A new variation of the blues that began in the late 1950s also became popular. The new style of music was called soul, and it blended rhythm and blues with gospel's exaggerated stage techniques and shouting type singing. The 1954 hit "I Got a Woman" by Ray Charles, an adaptation of the spiritual "I Got a Savior," became the template for soul. Charles said the song was a culmination of his search for several years for his own personal style of music: "Slowly I began to come into my own. Still trying to be my own man [but] I was trying to be accepted as me."[130] The song featured his raw, emotional voice and powerful piano playing along with backup vocals from a female group. Blues historian

Ray Charles brought a unique blend of rhythm and blues and gospel that became the music form soul with his 1954 hit "I Got a Woman."

Paul Oliver claims, "Soul [replaced] the blues as music that spoke for the younger generation of blacks, while it drew from blues for part of its expression."[131] Soul stars included James Brown, Stevie Wonder, Aretha Franklin, and groups like the Temptations and Supremes.

Despite soul's growing popularity, the blues continued to become more ingrained in the national consciousness. An example of its new, widespread cultural acceptance was the 1980 hit film *The Blues Brothers*, starring comedians Dan Aykroyd and John Belushi. Two years earlier they had done a skit on TV's *Saturday Night Live* playing Jake and Elwood Blues, white brothers dedicated to playing the blues. In addition to the film, they made several albums with accomplished blues musicians like Matt "Guitar" Murphy and "Blue" Lou Marini.

The strength of the continuing blues renaissance was seen in 1990 with the release of a new collection of Robert Johnson's songs. The singer who died in 1938 never had a song that sold more than five thousand copies, but blues lovers bought half a million copies of the 1990 collection of his songs. Two years later in Cambridge, Massachusetts, the first House of Blues restaurant opened. A decade later the national chain had a dozen of the restaurants that served food and hosted live blues acts.

White Blues

In addition to new white blues fans, an increasing number of white singers and musicians began performing the blues. Starting with British stars like Eric Clapton, many whites have combined the blues and rock and even dedicated themselves exclusively to the blues. Janis Joplin was one of the 1960s' premier female rock singers with Big Brother and the Holding Company. In 1969 Joplin formed her own group, the Kozmic Blues Band, and recorded a string of blues hits like "Try (Just a Little Bit Harder)." In *Blues for Dummies*, blues musicians and coauthors Lonnie Brooks, Cub Koda, and Wayne Baker Brooks praised the singer: "Janis was, quite simply, the greatest white female blues singer of her time or any time."[132] Joplin often cited classic blues singer Bessie Smith as her role model.

Scores of major white blues stars like brothers Jimmie and Stevie Ray Vaughan, Edgar Winter, and Bonnie Raitt, as well as the Allman Brothers Band, have been well received by blacks. Some purists, however, claim that the blues should only be sung by blacks because it is African American music. In 1993 Paul Garon, founding editor of *Living Blues*, explained why the magazine refused to run articles on white blues performers: "Only the very specific sociological, cultural, economic, psychological, and political forces faced by [African Americans] permeated with racism— produced the blues. *Nothing else did.* No matter who plays and sings [the blues] *black culture is an inseparable part of the blues* [and that means] the blues is defined *culturally* and not *acoustically*."[133]

Defining blues by virtue of the music's African American heritage renders any blues sung or played by whites an illegitimate form of blues. But Mary Christine Brockert, who was born in Santa Monica, California, and was known professionally as Tina Marie and the "Ivory Queen of Soul," strongly disagreed with that point of view. When someone once asked Tina Marie if she should be singing the blues even though she is white, she answered: "Overall

Eric Clapton and Robert Johnson

Perhaps no British rock star was more profoundly affected by the blues than Eric Clapton, whose introduction to the blues at age fifteen was a Robert Johnson record. Clapton in 2004 released *Me and Mr. Johnson*, a loving tribute to the country blues great in which the rock legend covered a dozen of Johnson's songs. In the album's liner notes, Clapton explained his deep connection to Johnson:

> It's a remarkable thing to have been driven and influenced all of my life by the work of one man. And even though I accept that it has always been the keystone of my musical foundation, I still would not regard it as an obsession. Instead, I prefer to think of it as a landmark that I navigate by, whenever I feel myself going adrift. I am talking, of course, about the work of Robert Johnson. [At] first it scared me in its intensity, and I could only take it in small doses. Then I would build up strength and take a little more, but I could never really get away from it, and in the end it spoiled me for everything else. Now, after all these years, his music is like my oldest friend, always in the back of my head, and on the horizon. It is the finest music I have ever heard. I have always trusted its purity, and I always will.

Eric Clapton. *Me and Mr. Johnson*. Audio CD. New York: Reprise Records, 2004.

In 2004 blues guitarist Eric Clapton released a tribute album that covered a dozen Robert Johnson songs.

my race hasn't been a problem. I'm a black artist with white skin. At the end of the day you have to sing what's in your own soul."[134]

The Ivory Queen of Soul's comment brings up another important concern about the blues—whether the blues is a particular style of music or something greater and perhaps more important to its identity.

What Is the Blues?

Booker T. Washington "Bukka" White would agree with Garon that the blues is African American music. White once said, "The blues came from behind the mule. Well now, you can have the blues sitting at the table eating. But the foundation of the blues is walking behind a mule way back in slavery time."[135] White, who gave his cousin B.B. King his first guitar, was correct that the blues owes its origin to slavery and the brutal treatment of African Americans in early U.S. history.

People who love this seminal American music often define it in ways that have nothing to do with its musical structure or its lyrics. Garon himself once wrote that the blues "represent a fusion of music and poetry accomplished at a very high emotional temperature."[136] The blues creates an emotional response in musicians, singers, and audiences that is as powerful as any type of music has ever created. Alan Lomax for several decades recorded authentic black music sung by workers, prisoners, and blues legends like Son House and Muddy Waters. Lomax's work was vital in preserving traditional blues songs and helping millions of people discover the joy of listening to them. But Lomax considers the blues as much an emotional as a musical experience:

> The blues has always been a state of being as well as a way of singing. Lead Belly [Huddie Ledbetter] once told me, "When you lie down at night, turning from side to side, and you can't be satisfied no way you do, Old Man Blues got you." A hundred years ago only blacks in the Deep South were seized by the blues. Now the whole word begins to know them.[137]

In Lomax's understanding of the blues, anyone can experience the blues even though the music originally stemmed from racist treatment of African Americans. And blues historian Paul Oliver believes the blues is "above all, the expression of the individual singer. Declaring his loves, his hates, his disappointments, the blues singer speaks for himself, and only indirectly, for others."[138] Oliver seems to be saying that the blues is about whatever people singing it want it to be, regardless of the color of their skin.

Ultimately, the blues means something different to almost everyone. Piano player Willie "Pinetop" Perkins once claimed, "What the blues means to me is trying to make a nickel and dime. They

Alan Lomax worked for several decades to record authentic black music sung by workers, prisoners, and blues legends. His work was vital in preserving traditional blues and folk music for millions of people. The recordings are housed in the Library of Congress.

Black Music and Black History

In his 1963 book *Blues People: Negro Music in White America*, LeRoi Jones tied the evolution of black music to the history of African Americans themselves. Jones's work theorizes that musical changes that had occurred in the blues and other music reflected changes in the way blacks were accepted and treated in a white-dominated society. Two of the recent changes in black acceptance were noticeable when the author reissued the book in 1990: The term *Negro* in the title seemed dated (*black* or *African American* is more acceptable today), and Jones, like many blacks, had changed his own name to reflect his African heritage—he was now Amiri Baraka. The book compares the development of black music from field hollers to the blues by claiming it arose from the status blacks had, including when most were slaves. This is the author's main contention:

> The most expressive Negro music of any given period will be an exact reflection of what the Negro himself is. It will be a portrait of the Negro in America at that particular time. What he thinks he is, what he thinks America or the world to be, given the circumstances, prejudices, and delights of that particular America. Negro music and Negro life in America were always the result of a reaction to, and an adaptation of, whatever American Negroes were given or could secure for themselves.

> LeRoi Jones (Amiri Baraka). *Blues People: Negro Music in White America*. New York: Quill, 1999, p. 137.

Bluesman Taj Mahal has played the blues for over fifty years. Taj says the blues is a living culture because the next generation will carry on the tradition of the blues—a unique music tradition that is 100 percent American.

didn't send me to school like they ought to. I haven't got good book-learning, so I can't get in no office. So I got to do the best I can do."[139] The blues to Perkins was a livelihood that spanned several decades and included a cameo role in *The Blues Brothers*. But perhaps no one has ever defined the blues better than the legendary Robert Johnson, who in one of his songs claimed: "You can call the blues, you can call the blues any old thing you please, You can call the blues any old thing you please, but the blues ain't nothing but the doggone heart disease."[140] He meant, of course, a heart that was sick with misery and not a physical ailment.

The Blues Will Never Die

Traditional blues is still sung, but the blues has also worked its way into virtually every type of modern music imaginable. That even includes rap. Music historians claim some spoken blues songs, especially the playful rhyming lyrics Louis Jordan made famous in the 1940s, were stylistic ancestors of this newest form of African American music. King, for one, believes the blues and their musical heritage will be discussed for many centuries: "When they look back five hundred years from now, hip historians will give the blues the credit it deserves—as the backbone of the American music."[141]

In his long blues career, Henry Saint Clair Fredericks, who performs as Taj Mahal, has seen the popularity of the blues fall and rise several times. But Taj Mahal claims the blues will never die, because someone is always falling in love with it: "Listen. This is our living culture. It's not going to go away. None of it will. There'll be echoes, and then a generation will come along and go, 'Wow.' They're always discovering my music."[142]

Notes

Introduction: The Blues and African American History

1. 107th U.S. Congress. "Official Proclamation." Year of the Blues 2003. www.yearoftheblues.org/officialProclamation.asp.
2. Quoted in Vladimir Bogdanov, Chris Woodstra, and Stephen Thomas Erlewine, eds. *The Blues: The Definitive Guide to the Blues.* 3rd ed. Ann Arbor, MI: All Media Guide, 2003, p. 218.
3. W.C. Handy. *Father of the Blues: An Autobiography of W.C. Handy.* New York: Macmillan, 1941, p. 232.
4. Paul Oliver. *The Story of the Blues.* Lebanon, NH: Northeastern University Press, 1997, p. 30.
5. Quoted in Giles Oakley. *The Devil's Music: A History of the Blues.* New York: Taplinger, 1977, p. 12.
6. Quoted in Oliver. *The Story of the Blues*, p. 7.
7. Francis Davis. *The History of the Blues.* New York: Hyperion, 1995, p. 112.
8. Quoted in Paul Oliver. *Blues Fell This Morning: Meaning in the Blues.* New York: Cambridge University Press, 1960, p. 113.
9. Quoted in Oliver. *Blues Fell This Morning*, p. xv.

10. Quoted in Paul Oliver. *Broadcasting the Blues: Black Blues in the Segregation Era.* New York: Routledge, 2006, p. 43.
11. Quoted in Oakley. *The Devil's Music*, p. 163.

Chapter One: The Birth of the Blues

12. Harry Belafonte. *The Long Road to Freedom: An Anthology of Black Music.* New York: Buddha Records, 2001, p. 14.
13. Quoted in Etienne Bours and Alberto Nogueira. "The Birth of the Blues." *UNESCO Courier*, March 1991, p. 27.
14. Quoted in Paul Oliver, Tony Russell, Robert M.W. Dixon, and John Godrich. *Yonder Come the Blues: The Evolution of a Genre.* New York: Cambridge University Press, 2001, p. 32.
15. Eileen Southern. *The Music of Black Americans: A History.* New York: Norton, 1997, p. 21.
16. Quoted in Earl L. Stewart. *Black Music: An Introduction.* New York: Schirmer, 1998, p. 44.
17. Quoted in Dan Gilgoff. "Making Music." *U.S. News & World Report*, 2004, p. 26.

18. LeRoi Jones (Amiri Baraka). *Blues People: Negro Music in White America*. New York: Quill, 1999, p. 42

19. Southern. *The Music of Black Americans*, p. 33.

20. Quoted in Burton W. Peretti. *Lift Every Voice: The History of African American Music*. New York: Rowman and Littlefield, 2009, p. 24.

21. Quoted in Oliver et al. *Yonder Come the Blues*, p. 32.

22. Belafonte. *The Long Road to Freedom*, p. 17.

23. Jones. *Blues People*, p. 142.

24. Quoted in Oliver. *Broadcasting the Blues*, p. 107.

25. Handy. *Father of the Blues*, p. 75.

26. Southern. *The Music of Black Americans*, p. 332.

27. Handy. *Father of the Blues*, p. 74.

28. Quoted in Peter Guralnick, Robert Santelli, Holly George-Warren, and Christopher John Farley, eds. *Martin Scorsese Presents the Blues: A Musical Journey*. New York: Amistad, 2003, p. 13.

29. Quoted in Handy. *Father of the Blues*, p. 75.

30. Quoted in Dorothy Scarborough. "The 'Blues' as Folk-Songs." Sacred Texts. www.sacredtexts.com/ame/cig/cig12.html.

Chapter Two: The Blues Go Mainstream

31. Handy. *Father of the Blues,* p. 93.

32. Quoted in Guralnick et al. *Martin Scorsese Presents the Blues*, p. 15.

33. Quoted in Alex van der Tuuk. *Paramount's Rise and Fall: A History of the Wisconsin Chair Company and Its Recording Activities*. Denver: Mainspring, 2003, p. 53.

34. Mamie Smith & Her Jazz Hounds. "Crazy Blues Lyrics (1920)." Just Some Lyrics. www.justsomelyrics.com/1760883/Mamie-Smith-%26-Her-Jazz-Hounds-Crazy-Blues-(1920)-Lyrics.

35. Oliver. *The Story of the Blues,* p. 105.

36. Quoted in Jones. *Blues People,* p. 129.

37. Quoted in Oliver. *Broadcasting the Blues,* p. 132.

38. Quoted in Oliver. *Blues Fell This Morning,* p. 46.

39. Quoted in Oakley. *The Devil's Music,* p. 84.

40. Howard W. Odum and Guy B. Johnson. *Negro Workday Songs.* Chapel Hill: University of North Carolina Press, 1926, p. 38.

41. Quoted in Oakley. *The Devil's Music,* p. 33.

42. Southern. *The Music of Black Americans*, p. 374.

43. Jones. *Blues People*, p. 17.

44. Quoted in Oakley. *The Devil's Music,* p. 84.

45. Quoted in Davis. *The History of the Blues,* p. 28.

46. Quoted in Angela Y. Davis. *Blues Legacies and Black Feminism: Gertrude "Ma" Rainey, Bessie Smith, and Billie Holiday*. New York: Pantheon, 1998, p. 42.

47. Jones. *Blues People,* p. 89.

48. Southern. *The Music of Black Americans*, p. 373.

49. Quoted in Jones. *Blues People,* p. 129.

50. Chris Albertson. *Bessie.* New York: Stein and Day, 1972, p. 133.

51. Quoted in Davis. *Blues Legacies and Black Feminism*, p. 138.

Chapter Three: The Country Blues

52. Quoted in Oliver. *Broadcasting the Blues*, p. vii.

53. David Evans. "Blind Lemon Jefferson." *Black Music Research Journal*, Spring 2000, p. 83.

54. Tom Piazza. *The Blues: A Musical Journey.* Booklet included in *Martin Scorsese Presents the Blues.* Santa Monica, CA: Hip-O Records, 2003, p. 47.

55. Southern. *The Music of Black Americans*, p. 376.

56. Stewart. *Black Music*, p. 9.

57. Stewart. *Black Music*, p. 9

58. Quoted in Oliver. *Broadcasting the Blues*, p. 68.

59. Quoted in Robert Palmer. *Deep Blues.* New York: Penguin, 1981, p. 107.

60. Quoted in van der Tuuk. *Paramount's Rise and Fall*, p. 113.

61. Oakley. *The Devil's Music*, p. 130.

62. Quoted in Oakley. *The Devil's Music*, p. 130.

63. Southern. *The Music of Black Americans*, p. 376.

64. Quoted in Oliver. *Blues Fell This Morning*, p. 44.

65. Charley Patton. "High Sheriff Blues." Harp Tab. www.harptab.com/lyrics/ly3244.shtml.

66. Quoted in Davis, *The History of the Blues*, p. 102.

67. "Blind" Lemon Jefferson. "Rising High Water Blues." Harp Tab. www.harptab.com/lyrics/ly2716.shtml.

68. Davis. *Blues Legacies and Black Feminism*, p. xiii.

69. Quoted in Oliver. *The Story of the Blues*, p. 111.

70. Oakley. *The Devil's Music*, p. 218.

71. Quoted in Vladimir Bogdan, Chris Woodstra, and Stephen Thomas Erlewine, eds. *All Music Guide to the Blues.* San Francisco: Backbeat, 2003, p. 292.

72. Quoted in Guralnick et al. *Martin Scorsese Presents the Blues*, p. 125.

73. Quoted in Alan Lomax. *The Land Where the Blues Began.* New York: Pantheon, 1993, p. 16.

Chapter Four: The Blues Move North

74. Tony Russell. *The Blues: From Robert Johnson to Robert Cray.* New York: Schirmer, 1997, p. 48.

75. Quoted in Guralnick et al. *Martin Scorsese Presents the Blues*, p. 240.

76. Quoted in Davis. *Blues Legacies and Black Feminism*, p. 183.

77. Big Bill Broonzy Lyrics. "Black, Brown and White." Lyrics Time. www.lyricstime.com/big-bill-broonzy-black-brown-and-white-lyrics.html.

78. Quoted in Jones. *Blues People,* p. 115.

79. Quoted in van der Tuuk. *Paramount's Rise and Fall,* p. 55.

80. Quoted in Guralnick et al. *Martin Scorsese Presents the Blues,* p. 25.

81. Quoted in Bogdanov et al. *The Blues,* p. 287.

82. Big Bill Broonzy. "Just a Dream." Lyrics Time. www.lyricstime.com/ big-bill-broonzy-just-a-dream-lyrics .html.

83. Quoted in Oliver. *Blues Fell This Morning,* p. 275.

84. Davis. *The History of the Blues,* p. 139.

85. Clarence "Pinetop" Smith. "Pinetop's Boogie Woogie." Heptune. www.heptune.com/pinetops .html.

86. Quoted in Davis. *The History of the Blues,* p. 137.

87. Stewart. *Black Music,* p. 59.

88. Jimmie Rodgers. "T.B. Blues—1932 Lyrics." Just Some Lyrics. www.just somelyrics.com/323648/Jimmie- Rodgers-T.B.-Blues---1932-Lyrics.

89. William Ferris. *Give My Poor Heart Ease: Voices of the Mississippi Blues.* Chapel Hill: University of North Carolina Press, 2009, p. 11.

90. Quoted in Arnold Shaw. *Honkers and Shouters: The Golden Years of Rhythm & Blues.* New York: Macmillan, 1978, p. 9.

91. Quoted in Davis. *Blues Legacies and Black Feminism,* p. 7.

92. Quoted in Oakley. *The Devil's Music,* p. 218.

93. Quoted in Davis. *Blues Legacies and Black Feminism,* p. 8.

Chapter Five: The Blues Evolve

94. *Life.* "Bad N----- Makes Good Minstrel." April 19, 1937, p. 38.

95. Quoted in Oliver. *Broadcasting the Blues,* p. 11.

96. Quoted in Davis. *The History of the Blues,* p. 175.

97. Muddy Waters. "I Be's Troubled Lyrics." Rhapsody. www.rhapsody. com/muddy-waters/the-complete- plantation-recordings/i-bes-troubled /lyrics.html.

98. Lomax. *The Land Where the Blues Began,* p. 408.

99. Quoted in Robert Gordon. *Can't Be Satisfied: The Life and Times of Muddy Waters.* New York: Little, Brown, 2002, p. xv.

100. Quoted in Lomax. *The Land Where the Blues Began,* p. 419.

101. Guralnick et al. *Martin Scorsese Presents the Blues,* p. 33.

102. B.B. King with David Ritz. *Blues All Around Me: The Autobiography of B.B. King.* New York: Avon, 1996, p. 106.

103. Quoted in Shaw. *Honkers and Shouters,* p. 62.

104. Louis Jordan. "Ration Blues." www .louisjordan.com/lyrics/RationBlues .aspx?l=1.

105. Louis Jordan. "Choo Choo Ch'Boogie." www.louisjordan.com/ lyrics/ChooChooChBoogie.aspx?l=1.

106. Louis Jordan. "Let the Good Times Roll." Lyrics Time. www.lyricstime .com/jordan-louis-let-the-good-times-roll-lyrics.html.

107. Quoted in Shaw. *Honkers and Shouters*, p. 63.

108. Arthur Crudup. "That's All Right, Mama." Lyrics007. www.lyrics007 .com/Arthur%20Crudup%20Lyrics /That's%20All%20Right%20Mama %20Lyrics.html.

109. Shaw. *Honkers and Shouters*, p. 32.

110. Quoted in Tony Russell. *The Blues: From Robert Johnson to Robert Cray*. New York: Schirmer, 1997, p. 78.

111. Aaron Thibeaux "T-Bone" Walker. "Call It Stormy Monday." Lyrics007. www.lyrics007.com/T-Bone%20 Walker%20Lyrics/Call%20It%20 Stormy%20Monday%20Lyrics.html.

112. Big Joe Turner. "Shake, Rattle and Roll." Lyrics Time. www.lyricstime .com/big-joe-turner-shake-rattle-and-roll-lyrics.html.

113. Willie Mae "Big Mama" Thornton. "Hound Dog." Just Some Lyrics. www.justsomelyrics.com/279960/ Big-Mama-Thornton-Hound-Dog-Lyrics.

114. King with Ritz. *Blues All Around Me*, p. 182.

115. Quoted in Shaw. *Honkers and Shouters*, p. xxiv.

116. Southern. *The Music of Black Americans*, p. 519.

117. Quoted in Shaw. *Honkers and Shouters*, p. xxiii.

118. Davis. *The History of the Blues*, p. 209.

119. Quoted in Shaw. *Honkers and Shouters*, p. 35.

120. King with Ritz. *Blues All Around Me*, p. 186.

Chapter Six: The Blues Resurgence

121. Quoted in Palmer. *Deep Blues*, p. 255.

122. King with Ritz. *Blues All Around Me*, p. 212.

123. Quoted in Lomax. *The Land Where the Blues Began*, p. 406.

124. Mick Jagger, Keith Richards, Charlie Watts, and Ronnie Wood. *According to the Rolling Stones*. San Francisco: Chronicle, 2003, p. 15.

125. Quoted in Gordon. *Can't Be Satisfied*, p. 161.

126. Quoted in Austin Scaggs. "Playing with His Legend." *Rolling Stone*, April 1, 2004, p. 41.

127. Davis. *The History of the Blues*, p. 108.

128. King with Ritz. *Blues All Around Me*, p. 240.

129. Quoted in Palmer. *Deep Blues*, p. 242.

130. Quoted in Stewart. *Black Music*, p. 223.

131. Oliver, *The Story of the Blues*, p. 18.

132. Lonnie Brooks, Cub Koda, and Wayne Baker Brooks. *Blues for Dummies*. Foster City, CA: IDG, 1998, p. 130.

133. Quoted in Davis. *The History of the Blues*, p. 239.

134. Quoted in Nekesa Mumbi Moody. "Marie Was a Powerhouse Per-

former." *Milwaukee Journal Sentinel*, December 28, 2010, p. B6.

135. Quoted in Oakley. *The Devil's Music*, p. 7.

136. Quoted in Palmer. *Deep Blues*, p. 19.

137. Lomax. *The Land Where the Blues Began*, p. xi.

138. Oliver. *Blues Fell This Morning*, p. 276.

139. Quoted in Tom Uhlenbrock. "Pinetop Perkins Reflects on a Lifetime of Music." *St. Louis Post-Dispatch*, March 24, 2003, p. C1.

140. Quoted in Palmer. *Deep Blues*, p. 106.

141. King with Ritz. *Blues All Around Me*, p. 294.

142. Quoted in Dave Tianen. "Taj Mahal a Well-Rounded Blues Scholar." *Milwaukee Journal Sentinel*, January 24, 2003, p. B6.

Chronology

1619
The first African Americans arrive in the English colony of Virginia.

1866
Slave Songs of the United States, the earliest collection of African American spirituals, is published.

1903
W.C. Handy hears a bluesman playing guitar at a train station in Tutwiler, Mississippi.

1912
The first songs titled "blues" are published, including W.C. Handy's "Memphis Blues."

1914
W.C. Handy's "St. Louis Blues," one of the most important early blues tunes, is published; World War I ignites the Great Migration as millions of southern blacks move north to escape racism and find better jobs in a war economy.

1920
Mamie Smith's "Crazy Blues" is the first blues record.

1926
"Blind" Lemon Jefferson's "Got the Blues" is the first country blues hit.

1936
Robert Johnson records "Cross Road Blues" and other songs in San Antonio, Texas.

1943
McKinley "Muddy Waters" Morganfield moves to Chicago and helps originate urban blues.

1944
Louis Jordan's "G.I. Jive" becomes a number one hit song; Jordan helps create the rhythm-and-blues sound.

1947
Muddy Waters makes his first blues record, and Aaron Thibeaux "T-Bone" Walker plays electric guitar on the blues standard "Call It Stormy Monday."

1949
Billboard magazine substitutes the term *rhythm and blues* for *race* to refer to black music.

1954

Elvis Presley records Arthur "Big Boy" Crudup's "That's All Right, Mama" to begin his rise to rock stardom.

1964

Country blues star Eddie "Son" House sings at the Newport Folk Festival, and Chester "Howlin' Wolf" Burnett appears on *Shindig* with the Rolling Stones.

1980

Release of *The Blues Brothers* movie starring Dan Aykroyd and John Belushi.

1990

The complete Robert Johnson recordings sell four hundred thousand albums in six months when they are released more than a half century after Johnson died.

2003

Congress declares 2003 the Year of the Blues to commemorate the one hundredth anniversary of W.C. Handy's encounter with an unknown early bluesman at a train station in Mississippi.

For More Information

Books

Peter Guralnick, Robert Santelli, Holly George-Warren, and Christopher John Farley, eds. *Martin Scorsese Presents the Blues: A Musical Journey*. New York: Amistad, 2003. A companion book to the Public Broadcasting Service documentary of the same name, the book has historic photos and interesting articles about blues greats and the music's history.

James Haskins. *Black Music in America: A History Through Its People*. New York: HarperCollins, 1987. A knowledgeable history about African American music.

LeRoi Jones (Amiri Baraka). *Blues People: Negro Music in White America*. New York: Quill, 1999. The author ties the development of black music to sociological changes in the status of African Americans throughout U.S. history.

B.B. King with David Ritz. *Blues All Around Me: The Autobiography of B.B. King*. New York: Avon, 1996. King, perhaps the best-known blues musician who ever lived, writes about his life, the blues, and the racism he faced while growing up in Mississippi.

Alan Lomax. *The Land Where the Blues Began*. New York: Pantheon, 1993. Lomax's book includes his discovery of McKinley "Muddy Waters" Morganfield and many other of his unique experiences in recording historic blues tunes for several decades.

Giles Oakley. *The Devil's Music: A History of the Blues*. New York: Taplinger, 1977. An entertaining, informative book about how the blues developed.

Paul Oliver. *The Story of the Blues*. Lebanon, NH: Northeastern University Press, 1997. The author of several books on the blues, Oliver provides a comprehensive history of the development of the blues.

Robert Palmer. *Deep Blues*. New York: Penguin, 1981. An interesting history of the blues that focuses on blues musicians.

Eileen Southern. *The Music of Black Americans: A History*. New York: Norton, 1997. One of the best books written on the historic development of black music.

Music

House of Blues: Essential Blues. Hollywood, CA: House of Blues, 1995, 2 compact discs. The thirty-two songs include historic blues tunes over the last century by male and female singers.

House of Blues: Essential Women in Blues. Hollywood, CA: House of Blues,

1997, 2 compact discs. The thirty songs include historic female blues singers like Mamie Smith, Memphis Minnie, and Koko Taylor.

Martin Scorsese Presents the Blues. Santa Monica, CA: Hip-O Records/Sony, 2003, 5 compact discs. This collection features blues greats from every era singing historic blues songs.

Robert Johnson: The Complete Recordings. New York: Columbia Records, 1990, 2 compact discs. This set includes every song recorded by the most famous and respected country blues singer of all time.

Websites

All Music Guide to the Blues (www .pbs.org/theblues/classroom/biblio web.html). This Public Broadcasting Service website offers definitions of various blues styles as well as links to other educational sites on the blues.

Bluescentric (www.bluescentric.com/ outside_sites.php). A site that has a history of the blues, biographies of blues greats, pictures, and other features.

The Delta Blues Museum (www.delt abluesmuseum.org/high/index.asp). This museum is located in Clarksdale, Mississippi, 1 Blues Alley, PO Box 459, telephone (662) 627-6820. The museum has displays on blues history and artifacts such as a small cabin that was the childhood home of McKinley "Muddy Waters" Morganfield.

Martin Scorsese Presents the Blues (www.pbs.org/theblues/index.html). Famed director Scorsese guided six other film directors, including Clint Eastwood, in making short films that explore the history and personalities of the blues for a Public Broadcasting Service series. Interviews and film clips from the films.

A Short Blues History (www.history-of-rock.com/blues.html). A brief history of the musical style's development and its link to rock and roll; it has excellent pictures of many blues greats.

Index

Picture Credits

Cover: © Terry Cryer/Corbis

AP Images/Matthew S. Gunby, 53

© Bettman/Corbis, 27, 47, 61, 69, 92

Bruce Glikas/Getty Images, 38

Chicago History Museum/Getty Images, 13

'Daddy' Dan Rice, introducing the song 'Jump Jim Crow', 1830 (engraving), American School, (19th century)/Private Collection/Peter Newark American Pictures/The Bridgeman Art Library, 31

© Don Smetzer/Alamy, 21

Frank Diggs Collection/Archive Photos/ Getty Images, 63

Frank Diggs Collection/Getty Images, 28, 33, 56, 65

Friedhelm von Estoroff/K & K Ulf Kruger OHG/Redferns/Getty Images, 83

Gilles Petard/Redferns/Getty Images, 41, 73, 75, 78, 80

Jeff Christensen/Reuters/Landov, 90

Michael Ochs Archive/Getty Images, 10, 22, 36, 42, 45, 85

Nicky J. Sims/Redferns/Getty Images, 93

Odile Noel/Redferns/Getty Images, 15

Paul Hoeffler/Redferns/Getty Images, 88

Robert Johnson Estate/Hulton Archive/ Getty Images, 50

© Terry Cryer/Corbis, 71

© Topham/The Image Works. Reproduced by permission, 58

Transcendental Graphics/Getty Images, 19

© V&A Images/Alamy, 66

About the Author

Michael V. Uschan has written over eighty books, including *Life of an American Soldier in Iraq*, for which he won the 2005 Council for Wisconsin Writers Juvenile Nonfiction Award. It was the second time he won the award. Uschan began his career as a writer and editor with United Press International, a wire service that provided stories to newspapers, radio, and television. Journalism is sometimes called "history in a hurry," and Uschan considers writing history books a natural extension of the skills he developed in his many years as a journalist. He and his wife, Barbara, reside in the Milwaukee suburb of Franklin, Wisconsin.